MICROTEACHING

Dwight Allen
University of Massachusetts

Kevin Ryan
University of Chicago

ADDISON-WESLEY
PUBLISHING COMPANY, INC.
Reading, Massachusetts   London
Menlo Park, California
Don Mills, Ontario

This book is in the Addison-Wesley
Series in Education

Material in the Appendix, beginning on page 126, is from *Teaching Skills for Elementary and Secondary School Teachers,* "Increasing Student Participation, Teacher's Manual, Teaching Skills for Secondary School Teachers." © 1969 General Learning Corporation. Used by permission.

Preface

Microteaching is beginning to be a rather widely known, if somewhat less widely applied, technique in teacher education and educational research. This book therefore seems necessary both as a means of informing those who have yet to hear of the idea and as a note of caution to those who see microteaching as a final answer. Our intent is to be candid, but inevitably we remain suspect as partisans. We have chosen a range of examples—by no means exhaustive—to emphasize the versatility of the technique. The questions that are raised by microteaching, at least at this point in its evolution, far exceed the answers it has been able to supply. Microteaching currently has the same promise, and the same danger, that newly devised research and training techniques have always had: the promise of opening entirely new avenues, perspectives, and alternatives to human exploration; the danger of locking in too early on a first alternative which arose purely out of chance and convenience. Although the idea of microteaching is incredibly simple, its arrival on the educational scene is quite late. Furthermore, the conception and development of this simple idea have followed rather circuitous, complex paths.

Microteaching was not dreamed up over coffee on a rainy afternoon. Nor did it develop full blown as a deliberate solution to the problem of practice teaching. Microteaching evolved slowly in answer to a problem that is common in teacher education. The liberal arts graduates who had entered the Stanford teacher-education program were reluctant to undertake serious study of the teaching-learning process. Most of the students had come for one reason: State laws required a teaching credential for school service. Stanford was a prestigious institution, and hence the study of education at Stanford was simply the least unattractive of unwelcome alternatives. The staff of the teacher-education program was understandably concerned that such attitudes might severely limit the amount that the students learned in the program. Schools of education have been on the defensive intellectually for decades, and we were making a genuine attempt to overcome both real and imagined difficulties.

To jar the students from their complacency, Kim Romney and Dwight Allen designed the demonstration teaching lesson described in Chapter 2. This was the forerunner of microteaching. The faculty originally involved in the development of this precursor of microteaching included Robert N. Bush, Dwight Allen, and Frederick J. McDonald, all of the school of education; A. Kimball Romney from the department of anthropology; and Thomas Gonda from the school of medicine. Professor Norman Boyan, who joined the seminar team the following year, took great interest in the evolution of the demonstration lesson procedure. Horace Aubertine,[1] then a doctoral candidate in secondary education, assumed a major part of the responsibility for operating the demonstration clinic and contributed heavily to the conceptualization of microteaching.

During the summer of 1963, the more than 60 teacher-education candidates in the intern program were randomly divided into two equal groups. Half of them got microteaching training, the other half the standard student-teaching experience in local cooperating schools. It was during this summer that videotape was first available to us. It was a research assistant, Keith Acheson, who first suggested using videotape, and we were fortunate enough to have available the prototype model of the original portable videotape recorder. Later we used the first production model of the same recorder. The wedding of videotape to microteaching techniques was a happy association, though it has since re-

---

1 Since getting his degree at Stanford, Dr. Aubertine has helped establish microteaching clinics at other institutions, and has continued to be associated with the development of the concept.

sulted in much misunderstanding of the role of videotape. Videotape is an important—but not a necessary—part of the process.

At the beginning of that first summer, every student was video-taped during a diagnostic five-minute lesson. Then, at the end of the summer, they were videotaped again. In addition, those in the micro-teaching clinic were videotaped periodically as the availability of the equipment permitted, given the ingenuity of both Keith Acheson and Alan Robertson, a second research assistant who shared in the task of harnessing this awesome technological wonder. The first technical skill used in the clinic was "How to Begin a Lesson," developed by Horace Aubertine in conjunction with Frederick McDonald and Dwight Allen of the seminar staff.[2] Through independent ratings of the second diagnostic session held at the end of the summer, it was found that micro-teaching-prepared teachers performed better than those with standard preparation, even though the total time involvement in the micro-teaching clinic was less than 10 hours a week, as compared with the 25-hour-a-week commitment required by the student-teaching experience.

The major structural change in the second year of the clinic was the addition of the repeat session, in which teachers taught an initial lesson, had a critique, reviewed the tape of their lessons—if a videotape were made, which happened in about half the lessons—and immediately re-taught the same lesson to a different group of students to see if they could improve. Several additional technical skills were investigated, including "closure," suggested by William Johnson, and "frame of reference," developed by Donald Wehmeyer.

Frederick McDonald and Dwight Allen received a grant from the U.S. office of education to investigate the use of videotape in the development of technical skills of teaching. The Kettering Foundation, in a grant to Robert Bush and Dwight Allen, undertook support of the microteaching venture itself. Early investigations were primitive indeed. We were foolish enough to ask such questions as "Does the use of

---

2   Barak Rosenshine later developed the skill based on the original conceptions of Horace Aubertine, but extended in a different way.

videotape make a difference?" The obvious answer, of course, is "It depends on what you use it for, and how." The videotape itself is not a variable, but at that time we were trying to defend the purchase of expensive equipment, and its use in teacher education, and our vision was not very clear.

Keith Acheson used the videotape technique to explore various styles of supervision, and James Olivero completed a study which sought to demonstrate that effective supervision was possible when videotape was substituted for live observations. It was during this year that microteaching began to be used for research. Jimmie Fortune made substantial contributions to research designs incorporated throughout clinic studies.

Donald Wehmeyer studied the effect of asking teachers to use multiple frames of reference. Bill Johnson found that learning could be enhanced if teachers were successful in obtaining student closure. Michael Orme helped to develop the concept of probing. David Berliner investigated various questioning skills, and the use of silence as a technique of classroom control. John Koran studied inductive teaching in a microteaching setting. Frank Sobol made extensive contributions to the development of several skills, pioneered the in-service application of microteaching, and suggested the development of a data bank of videotapes based on systmatic variations in microteaching sessions. Kevin Ryan developed various supervisory techniques for microteaching. Earl Seidman, Bill Fanslow, Barak Rosenshine, Tom Quirk, and Bob Lundgren were particularly important members of the clinic planning staff. David Young investigated lecturing skills and directed the videotape unit for several years. Kevin Ryan, Jim Cooper, Dick Clark, Philip McKnight, Robert Miltz, and Lewis Knight all served as coordinators of the microteaching clinic and contributed substantially to its design by suggesting experimental variables to be studied. Jim Cooper, David Evans, Dick Krasno, and Bob Pinney all developed applications for Peace Corps use.

In 1965 the curriculum and instruction professors at Stanford became concerned that the focus of the clinic was almost exclusively on general technical skills, which did not give them sufficient opportunity to deal with issues of subject matter. Professor Robert Politzer developed extensive adaptations for foreign-language teacher education. Professor Richard Gross, in addition to developing social studies skills, suggested a change in format that would allow a series of longer lessons to be taught to the same group of students, so that their programs could be charted and the teacher could gain a new dimension in his teaching experience. It was also suggested that several teachers collaborate on developing such units, thus giving the intern some experience in team teaching, with an opportunity to serve as participant-observer, watching another teacher teach a class. This so-called micro-class format proved to be an important addition to the development of microteaching.

We are most grateful for the contributions of the entire staff of the secondary teacher education office, as they held the hands of traumatized students, repaired scheduling errors, and kept the clinic in operation: Wilma Henderson Brady, Donna Wegner, Virginia Erich, Mercedes deSola, Gertrude Hayes Gannon, Harriet Emerson, Libby Morris, and Barbara Golden.

The term microteaching was first coined in 1963, but the concept has never been a static one. It continues to grow and change and develop both in focus and format. Our efforts have not been uniformly successful. For example, a number of attempts to use microteaching to deal with problems of discipline and control have been only marginally successful.

The vigor with which microteaching developed arose from the fact that it was a team effort, and at some point everyone in the group originally connected with the development of the concept made major errors. For example, Dwight Allen was at first opposed to the micro-class concept, feeling that it would hamper the development of technical skills. He could not have been more wrong. Other members of the staff objected to the original notion of the demonstration lesson on grounds that it was too unrealistic. As subsequent experience indicated, the demonstration lesson *was* too unrealistic, artificial, and stilted. But it was only after the demonstration lesson had been developed that the more realistic concept of microteaching emerged. Although those staff members who initially opposed the demonstration lesson were right, it is fortunate that their wisdom was not heeded. At the same time, it was this concern for realism that made microteaching a constructive teacher-training technique, an opportunity for real practice in teaching rather than the traumatic experience it started out by being. In several instances, research assistants who initially opposed the practice of particular technical skills later developed dissertations using those skills as dependent variables, and thereby contributed substantially to the refinement of the same skills. As microteaching became the focus for research, it led to research activities that changed the conception of such basic research variables as modeling.

As we developed the microteaching clinic, a number of new approaches to teacher education opened up. For example, as we were investigating ways to substitute videotape supervision for live supervision, we realized that looking at tapes of full classroom periods of 55 minutes was not only unrealistic but unnecessary. After we started using briefer time periods for our videotape supervision, it was a natural step to reduce the time requirements for live supervision, and from there to focus the supervision on one or two specific technical skills. Our whole model of supervision is a direct outgrowth of our work in the microteaching clinic.

Various drafts of this manuscript were read and thoughtfully criticized by Marvin Brottman, Richard Foley, William Lauroesch and Marilyn Ryan. Peter Wagschal helped prepare the research chapter. We wish to acknowledge also the contribution of our assistants, Lydia Elliott, Wilma Brady, and Nancy Kaminski, who helped us steal the time and paper to write this book. Finally, we wish to thank Estelle Buccino, who typed the first complete draft of the manuscript.

This book is written for a wide audience. To those prospective and experienced teachers who will be microteaching, this book should give an overview of the activity in which they will be engaged. To the many readers planning to be supervisors in clinics, the book should provide approaches to their tasks. For those teachers and administrators responsible for the training of teachers, both pre-service and in-service, it should offer tangible directions about how to set up a microteaching clinic. We hope that a good number of readers will come to the book seeking ways to adapt the process to the training of personnel for other professions and occupations. As we stated earlier, microteaching is getting to be well known. It is not known well, though. Although there have been quite a few articles written about microteaching, to our knowledge this book is the first extended treatment of the subject. In essence, then, the book is meant to be both an introduction to microteaching and a progress report on how far it has come to date.

Microteaching is intuitively appealing as a way of providing practice in teaching. It has come to be a convenient research locus which dramatically simplifies the logistics of investigating certain teaching skills and other learning variables. It is a means of highlighting teaching problems by reducing the complexity of the teaching situation. We hope that microteaching will continue to intrigue the imagination of people in the profession, and that it will indeed be a vehicle for unlocking new perspectives on the process of teaching and learning.

Amherst, Massachusetts D.A.
Chicago, Illinois K.R.
January 1969

About the Authors

DWIGHT W. ALLEN is Dean of the School of Education at the University of Massachusetts. Formerly an Associate Professor of Education at Stanford University, Dr. Allen is active in educational innovation, teacher education, school organization, flexible scheduling, vocational education and microteaching. Dr. Allen was one of the originators of microteaching at Stanford and has written several articles on the subject.

KEVIN A. RYAN is the Director of the Masters of Arts in Teaching Program and an Assistant Professor of Education at the University of Chicago. Before receiving his Ph.D. at Stanford University, he was a high school teacher of English and an instructor at the Naval Officer Candidate School. At Stanford he was the Coordinator of Supervision for the Stanford Secondary Education Project and the Director of the Microteaching Clinic in 1964 and 1965.

Table of Contents

Introduction

In the relatively short period of less than ten years, microteaching has been created, refined, and applied in the field. This is despite the alleged gap between theory and practice, between university thinking and the reality of the classroom. Perhaps we are about to enter a new educational era in which the efficient dissemination of educational innovations will become the rule rather than the exception. If so, education will be a more exciting profession.

In a national survey of student teaching programs in 1968, James A. Johnson of Northern Illinois University (DeKalb) gives figures which suggest that microteaching is used in about one-half (53%) of all teacher-education programs, including 4% which reported "extensive use." This degree of national dissemination has been achieved primarily by means of speeches, workshops, and mimeographed handouts, a feat that may be possible only in a jet age. This book should give additional momentum to the dissemination process.

The dissemination of microteaching has been so successful for a number of reasons. Let us discuss some of them.

First, microteaching helps to focus attention on teaching behavior and provides a setting for controlled practice. Attending to teaching behavior has been a long-unfulfilled need in the profession. Concentrating on *what* we do while we teach is a good place to begin an analysis of the teacher's job. The direct approach may be the secret to the success of microteaching.

Second, microteaching is a success because *it works.* Teachers and college students who are preparing to teach can get two kinds of satisfaction. During the initial experience they satisfy a natural curiosity to see themselves as others see them. The first few playbacks are irresistibly fascinating. These initial reactions are succeeded by perceived progress in teaching skill. Thus the second satisfaction comes when guided practice leads to improvements in teacher-pupil interaction.

Third—and this may be heresy to the educational establishment—the technique has been field-tested and refined without waiting for extensive and unequivocal research evidence as to its effectiveness. There is a risk involved here which the originators of microteaching and the authors of this book gladly take. It may be years before any definitive statements can be made about the overall effectiveness of microteaching. Such evidence will require replicated studies in which more-effective teaching must be distinguished from less-effective teaching. This will take much time and effort.

There is some research evidence, which is both consistent and promising, to show that microteaching does benefit college students who plan to become teachers. But without waiting for a complete, long-range analysis, many people—by their own testimony and judging from programs that have been carried out—are gaining new insights into their own teaching. Furthermore, the procedures and variations of microteaching are being improved, which should increase the possibilities of its long-range effectiveness. Possibly the teaching profession demands evidence of the effectiveness of a technique too early in the innovation process.

This book is an invitation to all who read it to join in the refinement and evaluation of microteaching procedures. To the basic sequence of teach-analyze-reteach, there are countless variations that need to be investigated. How can this sequence be changed? Perhaps other sequences are more appropriate to a particular insight. What is the problem to be investigated? The way we conceptualize problems to begin with has much to do with the way the subsequent investigation pays off. It is in this area that many opportunities remain unexplored. Microteaching is a tool of inquiry; yet there are no safeguards to prevent us from investigating the inconsequential. Which teaching skills should be investigated first? Second? And so on.

The point of departure of a program of self-improvement is largely determined by the person who seeks improvement. Yet some points of departure are more rewarding than others. Is it possible that the procedures of microteaching can be just as successful when videotape recorders are not available? The strategy of inquiring into one's own behavior should be independent of visual cues, yet having both sight and sound seems more attractive than having one without the other. How can microteaching be combined with other techniques of analyzing interaction? It is likely that microteaching will in the future be combined with other procedures in a "behavioral analysis clinic." To educators seeking a more potent curriculum for self-development, much remains to be investigated. The opportunities seem almost endless and the future offers an attractive challenge.

It is in this spirit of adventure that I commend this book to your use. Consider it a launching pad, a point of departure. Inquiry is most exciting when one's own behavior is one of the subjects being investigated.

Ned A. Flanders
The University of Michigan

To the women in our lives:

Carol, Cheryl, Carla, and Valera

Marilyn, Hilary, and Margaret

Chapter 1
Microteaching: What It Is and
What It Does

1-1 WHAT MICROTEACHING IS

A teacher holds up before four children a picture of what appears to be a branch that has five brownish leaves. However, when the students inspect the picture closely, they realize that two of the five leaves are actually butterflies. The teacher then questions the four students, trying to see whether they can come up with an explanation of this phenomenon. Fifteen feet away a supervisor aims the camera of a portable videotape recorder at the group, and occasionally jots down some notes. The lesson lasts for only five minutes, but during this brief time, two things happen: The students discover that the butterflies are camouflaged so that they look like leaves, and that this disguise protects the butterflies from their natural enemies. The teacher has a chance to practice the teaching skill of asking probing questions. As soon as the lesson is over, the supervisor has the students fill out a form. They do this quickly and leave the room. In the minutes that follow, the supervisor and the teacher discuss the lesson, reviewing the supervisor's notes and the forms filled out by the students, and viewing parts of the videotaped lesson. Then, after a short break, the entire process is repeated. However, the second time around, the teacher teaches a different group of four students. The teacher, the supervisor, and the students have been involved in the process of *microteaching*.

Microteaching is a training concept that can be applied at various pre-service and in-service stages in the professional development of teachers. Microteaching provides teachers with a practice setting for instruction in which the normal complexities of the classroom are re-

1

duced and in which the teacher receives a great deal of feedback on his performance. To minimize the complexities of the normal teaching encounter, several dimensions are limited. The length of the lesson is reduced. The scope of the lesson is narrowed. In microteaching, the teacher instructs only a few students instead of the normal 25 or 30.

A casual observer might describe microteaching as follows: A teacher instructs four or five students for a short time and then talks it over with another adult. An experienced observer would emphasize the fact that the teacher concentrated on a specific training skill or technique and utilized several sources of feedback, such as the supervisor, the students, the teacher's own reflections and the playback of video-tapes. The experienced observer would also note that the teacher has an opportunity to repeat the entire process by reteaching the lesson and again having his performance critiqued, and that in the second and subsequent cycles he teaches different students.

Fundamentally, microteaching is an idea, at the core of which lie five essential propositions:

First, microteaching is real teaching. Although the teaching situation is a constructed one in the sense that teacher and students work together in a practice situation, nevertheless, bona fide teaching does take place.

Second, microteaching lessens the complexities of normal classroom teaching. Class size, scope of content, and time are all reduced.

Third, microteaching focuses on training for the accomplishment of specific tasks. These tasks may be the practice of instructional skills, the practice of techniques of teaching, the mastery of certain curricular materials, or the demonstration of teaching methods.

Fourth, microteaching allows for the increased control of practice. In the practice setting of microteaching, the rituals of time, students, methods of feedback and supervision, and many other factors can be manipulated. As a result, a high degree of control can be built into the training program.

Fifth, microteaching greatly expands the normal knowledge-of-results or feedback dimension in teaching. Immediately after teaching a brief micro-lesson, the trainee engages in a critique of his performance. To give him a maximum insight into his performance, several sources of feedback are at his disposal. With the guidance of a supervisor or colleague, he analyzes aspects of his own performance in light of his goals. The trainee and the supervisor go over student response forms that are designed to elicit students' reactions to specific aspects of his teaching. When the supervisor has videotape available, he can use video-tape playbacks to help show the teacher how he performs and how he can improve. All this feedback can be immediately translated into practice when the trainee reteaches shortly after the critique conference.

Although we shall discuss many of the past and present applications of microteaching here, we do not intend to describe its limits, since we believe that the full power and range of application of microteaching is yet to be tapped.

1-2 WHAT MICROTEACHING DOES

To train teachers initially—and then to maintain their professional skill through a lifetime of service—is a tremendously complex task. Microteaching is hardly the entire answer, but it is a part of the whole, yet-to-emerge answer. The microteaching idea is basically a flexible one, and it could have a key place amid an array of training resources. There are particular areas of training to which it is uniquely fitted. Here, and in later chapters, we shall briefly discuss some of these areas and the usage to which microteaching is put.

Safe practice

As one teacher said: "Microteaching has added real meaning to our courses in educational psychology and sociology because we get an opportunity to practice what the courses preach."

Practice is, of course, a prerequisite for many learning activities. Much of a teacher's day is devoted to activities that are learned and can be improved through practice. However, almost all the practice in teaching is on-the-job practice, and for that reason there are severe limitations. Practice in the normal classroom, whether by a student teacher or by an experienced teacher, brings with it certain constraints. For one thing, students are there to be skillfully taught, not practiced on. Teachers are well aware of this. Practice must take place within a larger block of time. It must be integrated into the flow of the longer lesson. Also, the skill or technique practiced must fit in well with the lesson specified for that day. Most important, in the regular classroom, there is only limited opportunity for the teacher to receive feedback on performance. For the beginner, the student or practice teacher, the task is particularly difficult. He begins his practice by taking over the class of a master or supervisor teacher. He takes on the responsibility of successfully teaching an entire unit, and, to do this well, he has to utilize many skills and techniques. This is somewhat like learning to play football by being thrust into a scheduled game, without benefit of conditioning, of learning the basic skills, and of scrimmages.

Other professions have—built into their training programs—opportunities for safe practice. The law student has his moot court. The medical student has his cadaver and his rounds in the clinic. The aircraft pilot has his Link trainer. The actor has his closely supervised rehearsals. The beginning teacher, however, must learn how to teach amid the hurly-burly of his scheduled classes.

Microteaching was designed to provide teachers with a safe setting for the acquisition of the techniques and skills of their profession. The idea was developed at Stanford University in 1963. The beginning teachers in the Stanford Teacher Education Program needed a realistic training situation in which to practice before they took on classroom responsibilities. They spent the eight weeks prior to their initial teaching assignment in a microteaching clinic. A few years later microteaching was adopted as an in-service training technique. Experienced teachers used microteaching for similar practice purposes, but frequently adjusted the Stanford approach to fit their own needs. They used the practice setting of microteaching not only for skill training, but also to try out new curricular materials and instructional techniques. Both groups—beginners and experienced teachers—find microteaching a safe, realistic setting in which to develop professional competencies.

A focused instrument

One of the reasons that people have found it difficult to talk with any precision about teaching is that we approach it as an almost mystical phenomenon. Our discussions of teaching rarely get close to what a teacher actually does in the classroom. We speak of "the art of teaching," "the teaching act," and use other similarly vague terms. Granted, there is an artistic quality to some teachers' performances. Granted, too, broad universal terms are useful for some kinds of communication. Nevertheless, it would be valuable for teachers to have a more precise means of describing their activities, and recently some new ways of conceptualizing teaching are leading us toward this means: A more precise vocabulary for the specifics of teaching. Teaching has been analyzed as being made up of various types of activity, such as explaining, questioning, demonstrating, and so on. When teachers work within this new frame of reference and refine these categories of teaching activity even further, they can isolate the behaviors involved in certain teaching skills and make them the focus of training.

An individual teacher wishing to improve his performance can identify specific teaching activities and, by means of microteaching, practice them. Or a cluster of these activities can form the curriculum of a training program. In either case, the practice environment of microteaching allows teachers to work on the acquisition of *specific* skills; extraneous concerns can be shut out. To give an example, the teacher can work on a particular method of increasing student participation: redirecting student questions to other students. By enabling the teacher to focus on specific skills, providing immediate feedback from several sources, and then allowing the teacher to continue practice, microteaching leads to great strides in the acquisition of teaching skills in a short time.

A vehicle for continuous training

The twentieth century has brought startling and profound changes to our society. We can be sure that the remainder of the century will bring even greater ones. Teachers must be able not only to adjust to these changes, but also to deal with them in educationally sound ways. Unfortunately, the model for the training of teachers was built for another age, an age in which knowledge and culture were more static. The sheer quantity of new knowledge and the advances in the teaching-learning process are making the need for more powerful training programs all the more severe. We shall have to back up the old cliché of "teachers as continuous learners" with something more than lip service. Schools will have to take more responsibility for the advanced training of teachers. This will mean a major expansion of our present minimal efforts toward the in-service training of teachers.

After a few years in the classroom, teachers tend to settle down with certain patterns of teaching and instructional methods with which they are comfortable. In a sense, they reach a professional plateau and their development as teachers tends to level off. This is true of even the best teachers because they have very little incentive to improve, since their competence is already recognized. One of the reasons for the lack of professional development is that teachers have few vehicles for continued growth. Microteaching represents a partial solution to this problem. If teachers had a microteaching clinic as a part of the professional resources—like workshops and professional libraries—available to them, they could use it to systematically improve their instructional skills and to try out new curricular materials. Besides providing a needed practice situation, the clinic could also be used by teachers to demonstrate to their colleagues various teaching techniques and curricular materials. In a sense, it could be the setting for the professional dialog among teachers that is frequently absent from our schools.

As change accelerates and the demands for the continued growth and development of teachers become greater and greater, the profession must respond with a whole array of vehicles to stimulate growth. It is for this reason that microteaching's greatest potential is, perhaps, in the schools themselves even more than in pre-service programs.

Modeling instructional skills
Our classrooms have many outstanding model teachers, but the very fact that they are confined to classrooms diminishes their opportunity to exert their good influence on their peers. In a microteaching setting, good teachers can demonstrate their skills and be recorded on video-

tape. The basic structure of microteaching and its built-in flexibility make it a natural setting in which to develop instructional methods of various teaching skills and techniques. Teaching skills can be isolated and their performance highlighted so that the viewer can more easily identify the behaviors that make up the skill.

Well-executed models of instructional skills have numerous uses: They can be used as examples to be imitated. They can be used to show the instructional alternatives available to the teacher. They can be used to stimulate discussion about teaching. And, as we shall see later, they can be used as a major instructional component in a microteaching clinic.

A new approach to supervision

To most teachers, supervision is an unpleasant word. One reason is that people tend to confuse supervision with evaluation. When the classroom door opens and the teacher sees an administrator or department head standing there with his notebook, does the teacher at once think, "Good. Here is someone to help me be a better teacher."? Not likely. Probably his first thoughts are "Now I'm going to be evaluated. He'll be making judgments that will affect my future." Even when supervision is disentangled from evaluation, it is rarely performed well. As currently practiced, supervision tends to be generalized in its approach to the teacher's performance, infrequent, and negative in tone. For these reasons the teacher rarely initiates the supervisor's visit.

A microteaching clinic can provide both a good setting for and a positive approach to supervision. The approach is entirely nonevaluative. The stress is on instructional help to the teacher. Most teachers are rather sensitive about having supervisors sitting in the back of their classrooms. A microteaching clinic, though, is neutral territory. Since the students in the clinic would normally not be the teacher's, he is freer to experiment. The fact that the number of students, the duration, and the scope of the lesson are all reduced also seems to lessen the pressure on the teacher. Microteaching clinics tend to be very relaxed environments.

One of the key principles of microteaching is to focus on a particular teaching skill or some very clear objective. Whatever the aim of the microlesson, both the supervisor and the teacher are clear about it ahead of time. Therefore, in the critique period following the brief lesson, they are both ready to talk about the same narrow range of concerns. Instead of being all-encompassing, the supervision that accompanies microteaching is highly specific. Instead of having to wait to try out the supervisor's suggestions, the teacher can apply them immediately in a re-teach lesson. Instead of being negative in tone, the supervision is generally positive, since the supervisor, rather than evaluating the teacher's performance, is trying to help him in areas that are already identified.

A research tool

Microteaching was born of an experiment. From its very beginning, it has been used as a means of research. Many aspects of microteaching that render it valuable as a training technique also render it valuable as a research tool. Research in education is perhaps more difficult than research in any other field because of the many variables involved in the teaching-learning process. However, these many variables *can,* with the aid of microteaching, be sorted out. Many of the complexities of classroom teaching can be reduced, thus allowing the researcher to analyze specifics more closely. The researcher has great control over practice in microteaching. Variables such as time, content, students, and teaching techniques can easily be manipulated.

Any microteaching clinic, in addition to being a vehicle for direct research, is ideal for pilot studies. Before large experiments are tested in the schools, many of their "bugs" and problems can be worked out in the microteaching setting.

1-3 SUMMARY

This introductory description of what microteaching is and what it can do would not be complete without a caveat. As stated in the beginning of this chapter, microteaching is an idea. As such, it is potentially subject to misapplication and distortion. Most likely it is *not* appropriate to the acquisition of all teaching skills. Although it may make a teacher who is insensitive to his behavior more sensitive, it cannot transform a dullard into an intellectually exciting teacher. So unfortunately, it is not a panacea. It will not solve all our problems of professional training for teachers. More study and research are needed before we know its full potentials and limitations. Nevertheless, we believe that microteaching can provide the profession with a unique setting for training and for research in teaching. There are few teachers who would not benefit from the highly focused practice and feedback which are the basic components of microteaching.

2-1 PRELIMINARY EFFORTS TO TEACH SKILLS

The Stanford Teacher Education Program, before developing the micro-teaching clinic, experimented with various methods of providing teacher candidates with practice in teaching before they entered the schools.* Stanford's problem was hardly a unique one. One approach was the Teacher Aide Program, in which teaching candidates spent several hours a day in neighboring high schools, working with summer-school teachers. The intention was not only to have the beginners observe the summer-school teachers, but also to do some actual teaching under the supervision of skillful teachers. Although some beginners had very rich experiences, the overall judgment of faculty and students was that the program was inadequate. First, it was quite time-consuming, since the teacher candidates had to spend long hours in the neighboring schools. Second, it lacked focus; and although there were many expectations for the program, there was no way to ensure that they would be fulfilled. In short, it was difficult to maintain any "quality control." Third, it placed a heavy responsibility on the summer-school teachers. Besides teaching their classes, they were expected to give a great deal of attention to their teaching candidates. Fourth, the teacher

---

* The Stanford Teacher Education Program is a one-year graduate program for secondary school teachers. Before taking on the responsibility of internship teaching in local high schools, the participants spend the summer preparing themselves for their teaching assignments.

candidates often wound up doing little teaching and much busy work. It became clear that other alternatives had to be developed.

To overcome some of the inadequacies of the teacher-aide experience, the staff developed another approach: the demonstration teaching lesson. The theory was simple: Could we provide a situation traumatic enough to underscore the complexity of teaching, and thus give teacher education students the desire to learn instructional techniques? With this aim in mind, we established a situation which involved four students, each role-playing a typical student reaction. There was Eager, who responded positively and vigorously regardless of the travesty of the teaching. There was Slow Poke, who never did quite catch on. There was Know-It-All, who anticipated the teacher's stratagems, examples, and from time to time offered alternative approaches to the instructional procedure. And finally, there was Couldn't Care Less, who engaged in various destructive maneuvers, from talking, to noise-making, to the construction of paper airplanes, to walking out of the class.

The deck was further stacked in that the teachers were asked to teach a special game devised by the staff. The environment was manipulated, curtains drawn, lights turned off, the students placed at the extreme corners of a very large table, and a projection screen lowered over most of the blackboard. The traumatic situation was designed to have a dual impact. The first impact came from confronting the teaching situation. The second came from participating in a discussion the following day with the students who had served as role-playing conspirators the day before.

The demonstration teaching lesson exceeded our fondest and most perverse expectations. Most students failed miserably. Some able Phi Beta Kappa students broke down in tears. Failure hurt, but it was not nearly as painful as confronting the torturers. On the following day the students were able to report such dramatic statistics as the fact that 85% of the teachers forgot to turn on the lights in the classroom. Rarely did a teacher ever pull the students together into a teachable instructional group; rarely did a teacher exercise the prerogative of disciplining Couldn't Care Less, providing alternative instruction or explanation for Slow Poke, or trying to gain the cooperation of Know-It-

All. It was only on the day *after* the critique by students that the teachers learned that all the roles were solvable: that is, that Couldn't Care Less would always stop cutting up if requested to do so; that Know-It-All would become cooperative if the teacher gave any positive recognition of the fact that Know-It-All had already mastered the material, and that Slow Poke could learn if alternative explanations were given.

As training in humility the demonstration lesson was a complete success. It made the point that there was something beyond knowing one's subject matter that was a requisite for effective teaching. Substantially less effective, however, was the demonstration lesson's ability to help the teacher begin to cope with what to do about it. For the most part, teachers considered it too contrived, since they were teaching artificial material in a role-playing setting.

They found the exercise unrealistic because they felt little relationship between the game they were asked to teach and the content of their own teaching fields. The supervisors felt that it was difficult to help the candidates, since they usually made so many mistakes. Because of these limitations, the demonstration teaching lesson was changed.

In the next form of the exercise, the candidate taught a self-planned lesson, using content from his own teaching field. Again, he taught the lesson to role-playing high school students and the lesson was recorded. This time the demonstration teaching lesson involved teaching real material in an artificial situation. Although this version of the exercise was somewhat of an improvement over the preceding version, it was hardly satisfactory. It still did not seem realistic to the candidates. Many found having to teach a lesson and having to handle role-playing students simply too difficult. Further, the supervisors had trouble helping the beginning teachers, since in their teaching they used such a wide variety of skills and techniques, some applied well and some poorly. The supervisors found it hard to refrain from telling the beginners all that was right and all that was wrong with their demonstration lessons. One of the purposes of the exercise was to show the beginners how complex teaching actually is, and here the exercise was indeed successful. Also, although the beginners gained insight into the complexity of instruction, the demonstration teaching lesson did not seem to help equip them to teach better. What appeared to be needed was a practice situation in which real material was taught in a real situation. Once we decided to have the beginners teach short lessons of their own design to non-role-playing students, the foundations of microteaching were laid.

Teaching skills: an added dimension

In the first microteaching clinic during the summer of 1963, beginning teachers taught brief lessons to normal students. Usually they taught whatever they wished. Immediately after their lessons there was a critique period during which they received feedback from a supervisor and the students. Then the beginning teachers had a chance to reteach the same material to different students; this session, in turn was followed by a final critique period.

Although the microteaching approach was considered a major improvement over the demonstration teaching lesson and was quite popular with students, the staff felt that both the teaching and critique sessions lacked direction. Stated crudely, the "how-to-teach" dimension was lacking. Beginning teachers entered the clinic with the aim of teaching content and with little concern about methodology. They were confused when things went wrong. Supervisors found it difficult to give them the aid they needed in a short critique period. This situation was remedied, however, in the last weeks of the summer clinic during a research study by Horace Aubertine.[1] As part of his experimental treatment, Aubertine gave the beginners specific instruction in the performance of a teaching skill. The skill was set induction, a pre-instructional technique. Set induction involves preparing the students for the actual lesson, setting them up for learning with a dramatic introduction. Aubertine instructed the beginning teachers in set-induction procedures the day before they were to teach in the clinic. The beginning teachers were told to use the skill in their microteaching lessons.

As Aubertine's study shows, this practice of focusing on one teaching skill is quite effective. In light of this experience it was decided that subsequent microteaching clinics would be used to train the beginners in specific teaching skills. The decision was a pragmatic one. The beginning teachers needed certain skills prior to the start of their internship and the microteaching approach could accomplish this training.

The decisions as to what skills should be developed in the clinic were not made in light of any set of rules about what good teaching consists of or what teachers need to know, but resulted from the discussions and debates of the microteaching staff. In the last analysis, the skills that were chosen as the clinic's objectives were those that we felt would be of most use to beginners and that we felt could be effectively trained for in the clinic.

The viewpoint that did and still does imbue decision-making about the training objectives in the clinic is that teaching can be analyzed according to the types of activities in which a teacher is engaged. As Nathan Gage has put it:

Teachers engage in explaining activities, mental hygiene activities, demonstrating activities, guidance activities, order-maintaining activities, housekeeping activities, record-keeping activities, assignment-making activities, curriculum-planning activities, testing and evaluation activities, and many other kinds of activities. If everything a teacher does qua *teacher is teaching, then teaching consists of many kinds of activity.*[2]

Working from this basic framework and in fact refining the concept of teaching activities even further, Stanford Teacher Education Program staff members sought to identify, isolate, and build training protocols for critical teaching skills. We gave priority to the general teaching skills that seemed to us to be most important for beginning teachers to possess. This is not to say that we tried to force on beginning teachers *the* teaching orthodoxy, but that we tried to provide them with systematic training in a variety of teaching skills, so that once in their classrooms, they would be able to call on these skills as they saw fit. Rather than binding them to a particular approach, this emphasis extends the range of communications skills they bring with them to the teacher training program. The result is that beginning teachers trained in this way, once they are in their classrooms, have more freedom than those trained by earlier methods, since in a given situation they have a greater range of teaching skills from which to choose.

2-2 EXAMPLES OF THE COMPONENT SKILLS OF TEACHING

Although we borrowed heavily from the educational literature, when we started defining technical skills of teaching, we frequently had to make up our own vocabulary. The following skills are representative of the skills which we have tried to develop in our teacher candidates. These are general teaching skills that can be applied at many levels, for teaching many different subjects.

1. Stimulus variation

2. Set induction

3. Closure

4. Silence and nonverbal cues

5. Reinforcement of student participation

6. Fluency in asking questions

7. Probing questions

8. Higher-order questions

9. Divergent questions

10. Recognizing attending behavior

11. Illustrating and use of examples

12. Lecturing

13. Planned repetition

14. Completeness of communication

Let us discuss some of these skills in detail.

2-3 STIMULUS VARIATION

Boredom is a major problem in the schools. Students sit for long hours listening and watching instruction. The instructional styles of many teachers do little to relieve student boredom. Many teachers remain stationary at a desk or lectern. Many speak in a monotone. The pattern of student-teacher interaction is always teacher-to-student. Looking at these teachers as stimuli for students, a psychologist would conclude that there is too little variation in their instruction.

Perhaps the most effective way to help the teacher relieve student boredom is to affect the intellectual or cognitive component of the teacher's lessons. Getting the teacher to use more stimulating material and to use discovery-learning approaches also helps dispel boredom. Another way is to help the teacher change his behavior patterns, stressing behaviors that he can perform that will give his teaching style more variety. This skill training has been called, rather arbitrarily, "varying the stimulus situation," since its purpose is to help a teacher to become a more varied stimulus in the classroom. Teachers are trained in: *movement, gestures, focusing, interactional styles,* and *shifting sensory channels.* These behaviors can be trained for separately as individual problems become apparent; however, in the Stanford microteaching clinic, teaching candidates practice all of them at once. In order to integrate them into their own teaching style, candidates teach brief lessons and incorporate as many of these behaviors in their lessons as they can.

Movement. The goal of movement training is to break the teacher's habit of teaching from one spot and to encourage him to move freely about the classroom. As he instructs, he practices moving about the classroom.

Gestures. Head, hand, and body movements are very helpful to communication. The goal of gesture training is to get the teacher to be more expressive and dynamic in his presentations. The teacher consciously attempts to extend the range and frequency of his gestures, enhancing his oral communications with these gestural cues.

Focusing. Frequently, in a lesson, there are times when a teacher wants to call students' attention to a particular point. The act of calling attention to specific material we have termed "focusing." Verbal focusing is demonstrated by such statements as "Pay special attention to this!" "Look at the picture on page 71!" "Listen very carefully to this!" An example of gestural focusing is the teacher pointing to a specific object or banging on the blackboard for emphasis. In practice, verbal and gestural focusing are often combined when, for instance, the teacher points to a diagram and says, "Take a good look at this diagram!"

Interactional styles. Teacher monologs are frequently a cause of boredom. In fact, excessive use of any single interactional style can become routine and dull. The purpose of interactional training is to get the teacher to use a variety of interactional patterns. In the microteaching clinic the teacher is encouraged to practice three patterns:

A. *Teacher-Group.* The teacher carries on a dialog with the entire class. When he asks questions, he asks them of the whole group, and not of specific individuals.

B. *Teacher-Student.* The teacher directs a statement or a question to individual students. He may ask an individual student a question, receive an answer, and follow it up with a series of questions to the same student, trying, perhaps, to get the student to probe the issue more deeply.

C. *Student-Student.* The teacher, after asking a question, refrains from commenting on the student's response; or he answers a student's question by re-directing the question to another student for comment or clarification. Frequently the teacher is able to involve many students in a dialog without having to do any more than direct the discussion. Once started, the interaction in such a case is primarily among students.

The content and objectives of a lesson should dictate the interactional style used. Nevertheless, the skillful teacher should be able to use any of the above three patterns, as he desires. The varying of the interactional patterns should also result in a higher level of attention than would exist if only a single style were utilized.

Pausing. Actors and platform speakers well know the value of the pregnant pause in riveting attention of the audience on them. Teachers, too, can benefit from applying this device. During a lesson, the well-inserted pause can accomplish several effects. It can prepare students for an important statement or question, signal the transition from one thought to another, or stop the present action and rally the students' attention to the teacher.

Shifting sensory channels. Training in shifting sensory channels aims at heightening attention by systematic changing of the students' receptors. Put more simply, it aims to get the teacher to switch the primary mode of communication, whether it be oral or visual, so that the student is forced to change. For instance, when the teacher switches from oral to visual instruction, the student has to switch with him. The switch in primary receptors from ear to eye should sharpen students' attention.

The teacher who is sensitive to the possibilities for spurring lagging attention by switching sensory channels can vary his presentation in several ways. For example, for a lesson involving much verbal explanation, at several points he can switch to the blackboard or the overhead projector. If showing something on the board or putting something on an overhead projector and commenting on it does not have the desired effect of getting students to switch primary receptors, the teacher may try switching to the visual mode without reading it or further explaining its meaning. This forces the student to make the desired change from one mode to another. Having objects that can be passed around the class or having students manipulate some apparatus also helps to get students to change their sensory channels.

Training in stimulus variation strengthens the teacher's ability to attract and hold the attention of the students. In a culture that provides its young with so much powerful stimulation through such media as television and radio, it is especially profitable to teachers to be trained in this domain.

2-4 SET INDUCTION: A PRE-INSTRUCTIONAL TECHNIQUE

Observers have noted that teachers often spend little time preparing the class for an activity. Frequently they make the briefest of introductory remarks, if any at all, and expect rapt attention from their students. Training in *set* or *pre-instructional orientation* helps the teacher prepare students for the lesson in order to induce the maximum pay-off in learning. Set is more than a brief introduction. Its purpose is to clarify the goals of instruction, using student's present knowledge and skills to involve them in the lesson. Instructional set can vary in length and in elaborateness. It can take many forms: an analogy, a demonstration, or the posing of an intriguing problem the students can solve. In five-minute microteaching sessions the teacher can devote the entire session to establishing a set for a hypothetical lesson or use a briefer set for a self-contained lesson. In longer microteaching lessons the teacher can establish set and follow it by a full lesson.

Let us look at three examples of set.

First, the teacher begins the lesson by striking a large wooden match and letting it burn down close to his fingers before blowing it out. He makes the statement that what happened to the match baffled scientists for many centuries. He then asks the class if anyone can explain what happened to the match. This leads into a discussion of the principle of conservation of matter.

Second, the teacher reads an official-looking memo announcing that all Catholic students must leave school at noon because such children are no longer allowed to attend public schools. He then goes about a routine task like handing out homework while the message sinks in. After a few minutes the class is ready to study the topic of religious freedom.

Third, before having students write a book report, the teacher hands out a model of a very fine book report and a model of a very weak one. Both are reviews of the same book. The teacher discusses with the students the merits and weaknesses of the models, relying on the students' ability to spot them. Then the students are ready to start writing their own book reports.

2-5 CLOSURE

Closure is in many ways complementary to set induction. Closure is achieved when the major purposes and principles of the lesson, or a portion of it, are judged to have been learned, so that new knowledge can be related to past knowledge. However, it is more than a quick summary of the material covered in a lesson. In addition to pulling together major points and acting as a cognitive link between past and new knowledge, closure provides the pupil with the needed feeling of achievement. Closure is extremely valuable at the end of a lesson, and particularly at the end of a unit. However, it is also needed at specific points within the lesson so that pupils may know where they are and where they are going. If the planned lesson is not completed, the teacher can still utilize closure by drawing attention to what has been accomplished up to the point at which the lesson is terminated.

A summary of the discussion or an outline of the major points helps to bring all the elements of a lesson into a new unity. There is an important distinction, however, between instructional closure and cognitive closure.* Since cognitive closure is obviously more relevant, the teacher should check with the students to see whether they have made the all-important connections.

The following approach both helps the teacher ascertain whether the students have reached closure and helps students make connections between previously known and new material: First, review the sequence which has been followed in moving from known to new material. Second, apply what has been learned to similar examples and cases. Third, extend material covered to new situations. Although this skill can be taught in the shorter micro-lessons, it is especially appropriate to the longer lessons, in which there is a fuller body of material with which to bring about closure.

2-6 SILENCE AND NONVERBAL CUES

Critics of the schools have pointed out a common classroom problem. Gingerly stated, most classroom discussion is teacher-centered. Baldly

---

* See William Johnson's study (Stanford University Ed.D. dissertation) 1964: "Instructional closure is reached when the lesson is completed and the teacher has shown the link between past knowledge and new knowledge. Cognitive closure is reached when the students have reached closure and made the link between old and new knowledge."

stated, teachers talk too much. To get teachers to cut down the amount of unnecessary talking they do and to increase student participation, we can train teachers to use silence and nonverbal cues. The goal of such training is to keep the teacher from continually interjecting himself in the discussion and at the same time enable him to keep discussion moving. A related goal is to give students the chance to think about the teacher's or other students' statements. To accomplish these goals, we try to sensitize teachers to the problem of talking too much, give them instruction in several of the nonverbal cues they can use, and then allow them to practice.

Frequently, simply pointing out the problem of teachers dominating discussions is enough to strike a loud and responsive chord in teachers. Anecdotes can be very useful here. Another method is to show a few tapes of teachers who have set out to have a wide-open discussion and ended in teacher-monolog. Whatever the method used, getting teachers to recognize the problem is not a difficulty.

Nonverbal cues give students feedback from their answers without the teacher having to make comments on each answer; nonverbal cues also keep the discussion moving. We have identified four broad categories of nonverbal cues: first, facial cues (a smile, a frown, a serious or quizzical look); second, body movement (moving toward the responding student or adopting some type of "thinker" pose); third, head movements ("yes" and "no" nods or the cocking of the head); fourth, gestures (pointing to a student, motioning to go on or to stop, and pointing from student to student). Perhaps the most effective way to instruct teachers in the use of these nonverbal cues is to show them a model using these cues in a teaching context.

Once the teacher is aware of the problem and instructed in the use of nonverbal cues, microteaching provides him with a setting to practice leading discussions with a minimum of comment. He introduces a provocative question and quickly turns the discussion over to the students, trying to see how long he can keep discussion going without having to break in with comments. He is encouraged to stop students who tend to dominate the discussion, and to draw out quiet students. Teachers are frequently amazed by how much they can control the discussion without having to speak a word. The intention, however, is not to develop silent, wildly gesturing teachers, but to familiarize teachers with the many cues they actually have in their repertoire and give them a chance to practice using them.

2-7 REINFORCEMENT SKILLS

Psychologists have long been aware of the value of reinforcement in the learning process. Many good teachers know that they can increase students' involvement in their lessons by using encouragement. Frequently, however, teachers fail to develop their potential as reinforcing agents, or they get into the habit of encouraging only those students who are already doing well. Common, too, is the habit of using very few reinforcing statements from the full range available. Many teachers fall into the pattern of responding to students' answers with a bland "okay" or "good," regardless of whether the answer is a brilliant summation of an issue or a trite comment. Other teachers get into the habit of reinforcing only the exact answer they are looking for. In a search for correct answers from students, they unwittingly punish many students. The shy students and the slow ones tend not to participate for fear of what appears to them as failure. The wide-scale passivity among students, particularly in the lower tracks, testifies to the systematic discouragement students receive in our classrooms.

Before practice in the microteaching clinic, teachers are given instructions on reinforcement theory, and are shown a sample of the reinforcing comments and gestures that they have at their disposal. Also, they are shown a range of verbal reinforcement from "Excellent!" to "That's a good start. Now can you take it any further?" and the range of nonverbal cues from writing a student's answer on the board to the teacher nodding his head in recognition. Once the teacher knows the theory and is aware of the range of reinforcement he can use, he is ready to adapt these to his own teaching style. In the practice environment of microteaching, the teacher practices developing these skills and integrates them into his own style.

Supervision and video playbacks are very helpful in this case. Teachers frequently get so wrapped up in the content dimension of their teaching that they are unaware of their use of reinforcement. A skilled supervisor who is paying attention to the reinforcement process can point out to the teacher some of the opportunities to encourage students that he missed. This is as true for experienced teachers as it is for inexperienced ones. If videotape is used, the teacher can actually see himself doing such things as systematically ignoring some students or giving them only meager encouragement. The "students'-eye view" of the teacher provided by the video recorder can bring this lesson home forcefully.

2-8 ADVANTAGES OF THE COMPONENT-SKILLS APPROACH

The component-skills approach offers several advantages for the teacher himself, for the supervisor, and for the school or training institution.

The teachers

Telling a teacher that he should have more classroom participation and student involvement may be sound advice, but it is not always very functional. If a teacher knew how to obtain more participation and involvement, he would probably be doing it. The component-skills approach emphasizes the acquisition of one skill at a time. This is particularly helpful to the beginner, since by narrowing down the activities he should engage in, it makes his task much less complex and mystifying. If the training program can isolate specific skills and describe and demonstrate them to the teacher, the teacher is more likely to acquire these skills. For one thing, the teacher can discriminate these activities from what was previously a more general teaching-learning process. If the teacher recognizes the teaching skill to be learned, he begins to recognize the behaviors that make up the skill and the situational factors that dictate when it can be used. For instance, when a teacher learns the skill of reinforcing the students' participation, he learns what kinds of statements and nonverbal cues constitute teacher reinforcement and approximately when they should be applied to bring about maximum participation.

Once the teacher understands the characteristics of the skill, he is ready to practice it. By consciously practicing one skill, instead of just the general practice of teaching, he has a greater chance of mastering that skill. Also, the skill gained through this process becomes a teaching tool to be rationally applied. When the teacher has control over several teaching skills and knows that the effects of each are, the next step is to apply these skills to achieve his instructional aims. For this teacher the teaching act involves decisions about when and where to apply his skills. For the individual so trained, teaching is not a series of happenstances, but a series of professional decisions.

The supervisor

The component-skills approach gives the supervisor something specific on which to work. It frees him from a hunt-and-peck approach to supervision: searching for the teacher's weaknesses and then telling him where he deviated from good practice. When supervisor and teacher agree to work on the development of one skill, the vague generalities vanish. They are both operating within a common frame of reference. After a microteaching session, the supervisor and the teacher can concentrate on the chosen skill. This focused supervision makes it easier to decide what is and what is not good teaching performance. For instance, if the teacher is trying to achieve the skill of asking higher-order questions, the supervisor can easily record and categorize the teacher's questions. After the lesson, they have something very tangible to discuss.

Another advantage of the component-skills approach is that the supervisor can selectively reinforce the performance of certain skills and behaviors, while ignoring others. It is a rare sample of teaching in which there is no skill well performed, or at least in which one is not performed better than others. Applying the component-skills approach enables the supervisor to single out the well-performed skill for praise. This point is particularly important in dealing with neophyte teachers, who can become very discouraged by their early failures. When a supervisor can identify the skills they performed well and honestly appraise these efforts, not only is the teacher encouraged, but he is also more ready to deal with the skills that were not well performed.

The component-skills approach greatly simplifies the training of supervisors. It focuses the training of supervisors on specifics rather than on generalities. Instead of the supervisor's job being to deal with every problem as it presents itself, his job is to help teachers acquire the particular skill being trained for. Just as the trainee learns these skills in sequence, so too does the supervisor. As each skill comes up for training, the supervisor learns how to discriminate the skill and what constitutes good and bad performance of it. This brings up a related issue: With this approach, each supervisor does not have to be a jack-of-all-skills. It is quite conceivable that training schools might have different kinds of supervisors. Some could be master teachers with a depth of experience in the schools, skilled at dealing with a wide range of teaching problems. Some could have a very limited background in teaching—perhaps none at all—yet be highly sophisticated in a narrow range of teaching skills. This distinction between generalist and specialist supervisors could possibly make available to the profession an untapped pool of people to help us improve our professional competence.

The school or teacher-training institution

Frequently the behavioral objectives of a teacher education program, whether it be pre-service or in-service, are unclear both to those responsible for training and those receiving it. This allows for great freedom, but also for irrelevance and waste. The component-skills approach, however, forces the school or teacher training institution to define which teaching skills it considers important. It clarifies the expectation of all concerned. It also enables the institution to make a start on the problem of evaluation in order to more readily gauge the success or failure of its training.

Some may hesitate to choose this avenue of training on the grounds that we do not know all the skills of teaching. While it is true that we cannot pin down all the skills, this should not keep us from identifying and building training programs for some of them.

By breaking the teacher-learning act down into its components, we begin moving in the desired direction of getting a specialized vocabulary and a set of concepts that enable us to talk intelligently about teaching. As Dan Lortie of the University of Chicago put it:

My impression, after reading hundreds of pages of interview transcript, is that teachers possess very little in the way of a set of shared items or concepts about the subtleties of teaching, as an interpersonal transaction. The language they use is the language of everyday speech, and the assumptions which underlie that rhetoric are the common-sense assumptions used by Americans generally of similar social class and education. Unlike actors in the professional theater, teachers have not developed special words (such as timing and pacing) to catch and hold some regularities in the flux of performer-audience transaction. Unlike clinical psychologists, they lack a common shorthand to describe individuals and facilitate conversation with colleagues.[3]

The isolating, describing, and labeling of these teaching activities allows educators to move in the direction of greater precision and, hopefully, greater conscious awareness of what they are doing in their classrooms.

2-9 MODELING THE SKILLS

Microteaching's component-skills approach is used primarily to give the trainee a clear idea of the skill to be learned. The trainee has to know *what he should do* before he tries to do it. He needs some instruction before the practice with feedback in the microteaching clinic. Instruction in a particular skill can be given in a number of ways: by oral instructions, written directions, demonstrations, or a combination of these. In the early days of the microteaching clinic much of the instruction in skills was given to all the trainees at once, by a combination of demonstrations and verbal instructions. Although this approach was generally successful, the search for more powerful instructional alternatives went on.

Two avenues of research converged to give us our present solution of the instruction-in-skill phase of microteaching. We drew on the work of Dr. Frederick McDonald, who has been involved in the development of the microteaching concept from the beginning, and Albert Bandura; these men had studied the effects of models* in changing behavior. The second factor was the extensive research, by Allen and McDonald, in

---

* *Model*, as used here, refers to an individual demonstrating particular behavior patterns which the trainee learns through imitation. This use should not be confused with the word models referring to paradigms, as in the term "mathematical models."

the application of videotape recorders to the training of teachers. It was thought that if the demonstration of a particular skill could be recorded on videotape and shown to a trainee prior to his practice in the micro-teaching clinic, his learning of the skill would be enhanced. Therefore, we tried to record demonstration teachers in the act of performing a particular teaching skill. For instance, suppose that the skill to be learned in the microteaching clinic is reinforcing student participation. Then the demonstration teacher, in his interaction with students, tries to use a great number and a large range of rewarding and encouraging comments. Two patterns have been developed for the use of models: One is referred to as the *prior-practice pattern* and the other the *self-contained pattern*. When an instructional model is shown to trainees a day or so before they practice the skill in the microteaching clinic, this is referred to as the prior-practice model. This pattern is generally used with skills that have already been tested in the clinic. A day or so after the trainee has viewed the model, he teaches his practice lessons. Then he and the supervisor view the videotape of the practice lesson, and discuss ways he can improve his performance of the skill. Again using the skill of reinforcing student participation as an example: The two discuss how the trainee can increase both the frequency and the range of his reinforcing comments. Then the trainee is given a chance to view the model tape again, so that he can compare his own performance with that of the model. After a short period of time, he reteaches his lesson, trying to improve his performance by incorporating into the second attempt what he has learned from both the supervisor and the model.

A self-contained pattern is used primarily in training experiments designed to extend our present knowledge of the teaching skills. In this pattern the trainee comes to the clinic with no previous knowledge of the skill to be learned. The taped model is employed in a number of ways with different trainees, in an attempt to discover *which* pattern of exposing the model tape provides the most powerful training treatment. Frequently the model instruction is combined with other types of in-struction, such as supervisory help, written instructions, or self-viewing on a videotape. The use of the model in this self-contained pattern allows for experimental control of training protocols. Such variables as

Microteaching does not depend on video-taping. Even when they have no video-tape equipment, teachers (with or without supervisors) may take advantage of the controlled and scaled-down teaching environment. Recall, feedback, and rating are, however, facilitated by video-taping. One microteaching option is for teachers to record lessons for self-critique, without the presence of supervisors, and with or without specific ratings of technical skills. Supervisors can be invited to view recordings later, or they may be required to do so.

The Component-Skills Approach

amount of practice, degree of supervision, and frequency of viewing the model can be manipulated. This type of investigation is an essential part of identifying a teaching skill and developing a training package.

The use of human models in instruction is hardly new. Apprenticeship programs from the time of the early guilds up to the present have based much of their training on the use of models. The neophyte silversmith or carpenter was and is still assigned to a skilled craftsman. The apprentice's job is to watch the craftsman and model his behavior after his senior. Teacher education has used a similar approach for years. Most pre-service observation programs are based on the idea of learning by imitating model teachers.

Although there are similarities between using models in pre-service observation programs and using them in microteaching, there are also differences. One of the shortcomings of learning through models as used in observation programs is that this application is based on the oversimplification of the complexity of classroom teaching. Normally, the beginning teacher is given some instructions before observing a master teacher. When he sits in the back of the classroom, what he typically observes is a teacher performing several skills, many of them simultaneously. Also, these skills are often integrated into a highly individualistic style. Only the highly sophisticated beginner would be able to sort out the various skills and techniques from the model teacher's style. There is also the problem of confusing correlation of events with causation of events. An example of this confusion is the master teacher who discovered that all his student teachers pulled on their noses just prior to making a major point. When they all tried to analyze why they had developed this habit, they came to the realization that they had been copying the master teacher's nose-pulling preparations before making a big point.

Besides the problem of discriminating skills, there is little opportunity in most observation programs to immediately practice what is learned. Usually the student teacher waits weeks or months before putting what he has observed into practice. Then, of course, there is the problem of bad models. Although there are many effective teachers in our schools, not all of them are equally qualified in all skills.

It is somewhat sanguine to hope that beginning teachers will imitate only the well-performed skills of master teachers. Observation programs in which beginning teachers observe experienced teachers who either have a narrow range of skills or who are not truly proficient in these skills are programs that are working against their own aims.

The component-skills approach dictates that we break down the complex behavior of a classroom teacher and try to model individual teaching skills and techniques. The purpose of isolating the teaching skills is to simplify the learning task. Therefore, what is called for is as pure an example of the skill as it is possible to obtain. After observing hours and hours of tapes of classroom teaching to obtain some usable models of teaching skills, we realized that few measured up to our needs. While there were some very good examples of the skills we were seeking, none quite met our specifications. We needed examples in which the skill was well performed; in which there was a high concentration of the skill; in which the context was clear and the behavior was highlighted; and finally, in which there were few technical problems to inhibit ease of viewing. Therefore we decided to develop our own models of the various skills in a constructed microteaching setting.

The first step in developing models was establishing a clear definition of the skill we were trying to demonstrate. Then we sought to model the skill in a very short teaching situation. The procedures used in developing models are similar to the normal procedures of microteaching. The model was taped; immediately afterward the model teacher and an advisory group viewed the tape to see how the performance of the skill could be sharpened and improved. It was then taught again, with the model teacher trying to incorporate the suggestions. This procedure was repeated over and over, frequently changing groups of students until a satisfactory model of performance of the skill was captured on tape.

Sound film is the ideal medium for presenting models of the technical skill of teaching. However, the portable videotape recorder has many strengths in the development and display of models. First, in the development of models, the portable videotape recorder can be taken to the best setting available for the demonstration. Second, the tape is reusable, which means that, in the attempt to get one usable model, several demonstration sessions can be taped with little or no waste. Third, the tapes can be reviewed to show the model teacher his performance and to help him improve. Some of these advantages are also relevant to the display of the model to the trainee. First, the model tape can be brought to the setting in which microteaching is taking place. Second, the model tape can be stopped at any point for discussion with the trainee and sections can be replayed over and over. Also, videotapes, like audiotapes, can be reproduced, and several copies of a model can be made available. Another display advantage is that the actual model lesson can be preceded or followed by a commentary on the skill. Instructions relating to what to look for or principles of classroom application of the skill can accompany the actual model.

Some unanswered questions

The use of models for instruction in classroom teaching skills is very much in the development stage. There are still many unanswered questions about the appropriate use of models. For example, what types of skills and teaching behaviors are best learned through modeling? Are certain personalities more influenced by models than others? After the trainee has viewed the model, how much practice—if any—is necessary for the training to be transferred? In order for models to be most effective, must the model be of the same sex as the trainee? Must the model be teaching the same subject matter? Does a large age difference between model and trainee make any difference? Another important question concerns the application of the skill-to-be-learned in the classroom: Can we simultaneously train performance of the skill and decision-making regarding the application of it in the classroom? These are all research questions, and it is clear that there is much research to be done in this area.

2-10 SUMMARY

The use of highly particularized models of skills is consistent with the general approach of microteaching. Modeling is the natural instructional counterpart of the practice dimension of microteaching. As teachers do in microteaching, the models try to filter the complexity out of teaching. Both methods are short and concentrated. Both focus on one skill or a cluster of related ones. Both work on the principle of highlighting and sometimes exaggerating teaching behaviors.

The use of models in teaching skills could have a major impact on pre-service and in-service training. Seeing a demonstration in which a particular skill is highlighted appears to have much more transfer quality than the other alternatives of verbal or written instructions. The quality of high definition that is basic to a good model makes initial understanding and appreciation of the skill much easier for the trainee. Finally, the fact that the models are filmed or taped enables the learner to view the model as often as possible. He can look at the model as often as he needs. The future development of a broad range of models for the component skills of teaching could provide teachers not only with a deepened understanding of good teaching, but also a standard by which to gauge their own performances.

REFERENCES

1. Aubertine, Horace E., *An Experiment in the Set Induction Process and Its Application in Teaching.* Unpublished doctoral dissertation, School of Education, Stanford University, 1964; 140 pages.

2. Gage, Nathan, "Theories of Teaching," *NSSE Yearbook,* edited by Ernest R. Hilgard (Chicago, 1963), page 275

3. Lortie, Dan C., "Teacher Socialization: The Robinson Crusoe Syndrome," *The Real World of the Beginning Teacher,* Washington, D.C.: NEA, 1966, page 58

Chapter 3
The Elements of Microteaching

The true test of any idea is the translating of it into reality. We hope that this chapter will be a practical guide for those interested in translating the idea of microteaching into a functioning clinic for practice in teaching. The chapter deals with a range of topics, from decisions to software, but it does more than simply catalog the various elements of a microteaching clinic. It tries to give the reader some sense of the issues and problem of implementation. The story of microteaching has not been one long success story. As with any new venture, there have been fumblings and frustrations. In the interests of preserving the sanity and the realistic perspective of those who would establish a microteaching clinic, we want to pass on the fruits of our trial-and-error learning.

When one tries to add flesh and blood to the bones of the microteaching clinic, one runs into problems. As stated earlier, microteaching is a very elastic idea. It can be applied by a small number of teachers who are looking for a means to improve their teaching ability, or it can be used by a large university as a major segment of training for all its pre-service teachers. Given this dilemma of just how to give concrete form to what is basically an abstraction, we have chosen to steer a cautious path. Although we address ourselves to the general issues and problems of implementing a microteaching clinic, we draw heavily on our own experience at Stanford University. The Stanford Microteaching Clinic was designed to provide training and practice in basic instructional skills for 150 pre-service teacher-candidates. The reader is warned, therefore, that each user must adapt microteaching to his own situation and needs.

We realize, too, that we are bound by our own experience and that of our colleagues. This volume represents an initial description of what appears to be a very promising training procedure. As such, it is not designed to impose orthodoxy on the application of this process. It is our hope, as we said before, that the reader will discover extensions, implications, and shortcuts that our myopia prevents our seeing at this time.

3-1 DECISIONS

To say that the results of a microteaching clinic depend primarily on the decisions made prior to the clinic's operation is to state the obvious. Obvious though it may be, however, the point cannot be stressed enough. Long before the clinic is established, the responsible parties must sit down and make a series of primary and secondary decisions.

Primary decisions

The primary decisions involve purposes and objectives. The most fundamental decision concerns the microteaching clinic's purposes. Is it the purpose of the clinic to train people in already identified skills and techniques? Shall the clinic be used as a research tool to identify technical skills of teaching? Shall it be used to investigate other aspects of the teaching process? Should the clinic be used for a combination of these purposes, and, if so, in what proportions?

The next set of decisions deals with the specific objectives of the clinic. Who is to be trained and how will they use the training? What are the skills, techniques, strategies—the terminal behaviors—which the clinic will help bring about? Where will the microteaching clinic fit in the overall program of training?

Another set of decisions concerns the instructional component and evaluation. How will the trainees be instructed in the skills and techniques to be practiced in the clinic? Will they receive live demonstrations? Will they have written instructions? Will they see model tapes of the behaviors? How will the overall results of the clinic be evaluated? What kinds of follow-up to the microteaching training will the trainees receive?

Secondary decisions

The secondary decisions, although not of the same degree of importance as the primary ones, are nonetheless crucial. The loftiest objectives can be sabotaged by weak decision-making at this level. Here are some of the secondary decisions that must be made: Who will do the supervising in microteaching? What kinds of training will they receive? How many students will be needed for the microteaching clinic? How many will be taught during a micro-lesson? According to what criteria will the students be grouped? Will they be paid, and if so, how much? How long will a micro-lesson be? Will micro-lessons vary in length according to the skill to be learned? How long will a critique period be? What methods of feedback will be used? Will students fill out written feedback forms or will their feedback be given verbally? Will videotape recorders be used? If so, how often? Which taped lessons will be saved?

Then there are other questions, unique to each institution. If a microteaching clinic is to be used in a college or university setting, what credit will be given for participation in it? Will participation in the clinic be voluntary or a program requirement? If used in a school, will the participants receive in-service credit? Will time be made available to participate in the clinic?

Another group of decisions involves space and facilities. Given the number of trainees and the time limitations, how many microteaching sites or stations will be needed? How many will have videotape recorders? Will special rooms be needed for the students when they are not being taught? What special arrangements need to be made for such subjects as natural science and physical education?

Then there are several decisions regarding personnel. These decisions, of course, depend on the size and scope of the clinic. For a small operation, one or two people can fill all the necessary roles. For a large training program, a special staff will be needed. Who will oversee the day-to-day operations of the microteaching clinic? Who will make out the schedules? Who will train the supervisors? Who will take charge of the initial skill-training sessions? Who will recruit and train the students? If videotape recorders are to be used, who will train the technicians and oversee the videotape recorder operations?

The actual making of these decisions should not be put off to the last minute. Their importance underlines the need for careful and thorough pre-planning. The larger the microteaching clinic, in terms of personnel involved and length of operation, the greater the possibilities for mix-ups and breakdowns. At Stanford we normally began planning two or three months before the clinic began, and we found a strong correlation between the efficiency of the clinic and the care taken in working through these decisions in pre-planning sessions.

In this and subsequent chapters, we shall give some indication of how these questions and others were answered in our own case. However, any setting in which a microteaching clinic is established will have unique problems, and unique answers will have to be generated.

3-2 STRUCTURE

Once the major purposes and specific objectives of a microteaching clinic have been decided on, basic structural considerations must be dealt with. When all the above decisions have been made, the job is to utilize them to shape a realistic and efficient structure. Since a microteaching clinic is typically set in an ongoing institution, many competing factors have to be considered in building a structure. Here are some of these competing factors: teaching loads or course demands of the trainees; other duties and time requirements of supervisory personnel; availability of students, and (if videotape recorders are used) of operators; other scheduling demands of the rooms used for microteaching. As in every human undertaking, compromises have to be made as we move from the ideal to the possible.

Those who build this structure must be sensitive to human weakness and fallibility. This is a point that is frequently ignored in pre-planning sessions. However, the overall structure must be realistic, in the sense that it takes the human factors into account. For instance, in spite of all the lists, schedules, and memoranda sent out, people will still occasionally become sick, show up late, and forget appointments. Then there is fatigue. What may appear to be a tightly organized structure that uses every bit of time may, in fact, be totally unworkable. It may not take into consideration the fact that students get tired and sometimes need the adolescent equivalent of a coffee break. Also, there are the small procedural problems—like running out of feedback forms or equipment breaking down—which, although trivial with respect to the overall objectives, can become major stumbling blocks to the people trying to run a tidy ship. The only answer here is to give the microteaching staff a sense of perspective of the total operation. The fundamental objective of the clinic is to provide practice in teaching, and this objective should be uppermost in the staff's minds. The annoying obstacles should not deter them from fulfilling these objectives.

A major problem in a large clinic can result from not keeping to the schedule. The daily schedule simply states to teachers and supervisors, "who, where, and when." The schedule symbolically represents that clinic's structure. Deviations from the schedule thus endanger the total structure. The problem of getting off-schedule is singled out here because of the frustrating experience of the staff in the first large microteaching clinic. Four years ago the clinic was expanded to train 140 pre-service teachers. Sixteen supervisors and forty students were involved. The clinic was set up to operate from 8 o'clock in the morning until noon. In the first weeks of operation the clinic was running until 1:00 and 2:00 P.M. Trainees were kept waiting. Supervisors were forced to miss classes and appointments. The morale of the trainees and supervisors was very low. Only the students, who worked on an hourly basis, were happy. The cause of all this difficulty turned out to be two or three well-intentioned supervisors. They had fallen into the habit of allowing their trainees to teach longer than the specified time. They tended to stretch the ten-minute critique session to 15 and 20 minutes. This, of course, caused a ripple effect. The students who were kept longer were late for their next assignment and slowed up another waiting trainee and supervisor. This delay affected the subsequent assignment, since no one was about to shorten the teaching or critique time. Soon there were two or three trainees lined up outside each station and inside there was a supervisor and a trainee waiting for students to show up. The solution or this problem was a simple one. One iron rule was made: *The schedule is the law.* Supervisors, trainees, and students were told that the schedule could not be violated. If someone were late or a station got behind schedule, the session was canceled and rescheduled for another time. Once this rule was announced and made operative, the clinic began running smoothly and the morale of all concerned improved.

What this means is that besides developing a structure that takes into consideration the human factor, one must also have strategies to handle daily problems. There should be one person who is responsible for making daily decisions about the clinic. He should be the one the clinic personnel go to with requests and complaints. When a session has to be canceled, he should do it, and there should be a block of free time into which he can reschedule the canceled session. In short, building the structure is not enough, particularly in the beginning when the micro-teaching personnel are inexperienced. There must also be a trouble-shooter, armed with strategies to keep the clinic moving.

One final comment on building a structure: A large microteaching clinic, like the one at Stanford, represents a substantial investment of time and money. The structure should be efficient in its use of human and machine resources. For instance, it is wasteful to schedule super-visors to work in the clinic at times spread out through the day rather than for a block of two or three hours. Similarly, microteaching students should be assigned in such a way that they are not faced with long periods of free time.

3-3 PATTERNS OF TRAINING

The training and practice in the clinic must be organized to facilitate the clinic's objectives. Three patterns of training have been developed at Stanford: (1) The micro-lesson. This is a short five-minute lesson, used primarily to train for single teaching skills. (2) The micro-class. This is a longer, twenty-minute lesson, which is part of an instructional unit and which is group-planned and executed. (3) The research clinical sessions. These are self-contained training sessions which are used to test new training protocols and extend our knowledge of teaching skills. Al-though microteaching goes on at other times during the year, these three patterns of training are organized during the eight weeks of sum-mer session as part of the overall pre-service training of teachers.

The micro-lesson

The five-minute lesson fits into a framework of a week's emphasis on a particular skill. A typical pattern is as follows. The trainees receive a live or tape demonstration of the skill to be used in their five-minute lessons throughout the week. Opportunities are given for them to get clarifications of the purpose and uses of the skill in a classroom. Then each trainee is scheduled for two 45-minute sequences during the week. A sequence begins with the trainee teaching a brief lesson he has developed to stress some concept or principle. He usually teaches this lesson to three or four students. The supervisor is present in the rear of the room; when possible, the lesson is videotaped. After the trainee has taught for four minutes, the video technician, or the supervisor, gives him a signal indicating that he has one more minute. The signal can be either the snapping of the fingers or a visual cue of some kind. After the lesson the supervisor hands out rating forms to the students and the supervisor fills one out himself. Since the rating forms are simple and familiar to the students, this rarely takes longer than a minute or so. When the students have finished rating and handed their forms to the supervisor, they leave the room. In the meantime, the teacher-trainee collects his materials and readies the room for the next trainee. Normally the supervisor tries to get the trainee to estimate his success with respect to the particular skill being worked on. Then they move on to the students' and supervisor's rating reports, which deal with aspects of the skill to be learned.

During the critique period the trainee and supervisor center their discussion on the performance of the skill and occasionally on one other item which the trainee is interested in improving. When a video-tape recording is available, pertinent parts of it are gone over. The intention of the critique period is to help the trainee think of ways of improving his performance for the next teaching session, which will follow shortly. The supervisor's main objectives are to help the trainee think and to offer alternative approaches. At the end of the 10-minute critique period the trainee leaves the room for a 15-minute planning period. During this time he is expected to recast his lesson in the light of the suggestions of the supervisor and the students and particularly his own fresh thoughts. While the trainee is rethinking his lesson, the supervisor is going through a 15-minute teach-critique cycle with another trainee.

After the planning break the first trainee begins the second phase: the reteach session. He teaches the same basic lesson, not to the original three or four students, but to a new group of students at the same grade level as the first. At the end of the lesson the same procedures are followed. Rating forms are filled out and parts of the videotape are viewed. The supervisor helps the trainee to evaluate his progress from teach to reteach session, and suggests ways that the skill could be further improved. Then the second trainee begins his reteach session. The entire pattern from "first teach" to second critique takes 45 minutes.

Two days later the trainee returns to the clinic and repeats the 45-minute pattern of teach, critique, planning, reteach and recritique. Although the trainee develops and teaches a different lesson, he works on the performance of the same skill. This particular pattern of five-minute lessons allows the trainee to practice each skill four times under conditions of maximum feedback, and it has been found to be quite adequate for most of the trainees for most of the skills. When a trainee has trouble with a particular skill, however, special arrangements are made. The supervisor schedules extra microteaching time for him. Normally, one day a week is set aside for make-up work and extra training sessions.

Many are shocked at the brief period of time allowed for practice in the micro-lesson. A common question is "What could possibly be taught in five minutes?" Since this question most frequently comes from college and high school teachers, one could surmise that these groups have been conditioned to think that knowledge comes in 45- or 50-minute chunks. Still, most people, when they encounter microteaching for the first time, are constantly wanting to increase the class size and length of lesson.

A number of formal and informal experiments in this regard produced the consistent result that *time is not really a very important variable.* Specifically, we looked at the difference between 4- and 7-minute lessons, and found no detectable differences. Perhaps there is a universal phenomenon that holds in the microteaching world as well as in the actual classroom: A teacher with 4 minutes wants 5, and one with 5 would like 7, and one with 7 would like 10, and one with 10 would be more comfortable with 15. Is this not reminiscent of the teacher with 40 minutes? He wants 45. And with 45, he wants 50 minutes, and with 50 minutes he is sure that 55 would be even better. We pay entirely too much attention to the variable of time in American education at all levels, microteaching included. The only real evidence we have to back up this opinion is that our trainees have rarely found the 5-minute lesson a great limitation.

Our insistence on adhering to the 5-minute micro-lesson pattern would seem arbitrary indeed, however, if all we could say for it was that our students could adjust to it. The length of the micro-lesson follows from its purpose. Recall that one of the major purposes of the clinic is to provide training in selected teaching skills. And although the short micro-lesson is not suitable for the practice of all skills, for many this time period seems ideal. Microteaching is designed to be a highly focused, highly concentrated experience. Five minutes of practice of a selected skill gives both the trainee and the supervisor much grist for the mill. The short teaching experience, as opposed to a longer session, allows for a greater possibility of recall of specific instances of the skill performance.

Looked at from another perspective, the short period of time allows little opportunity for extraneous problems to muddy the water. In longer microteaching lessons, of 10 minutes or more, the trainee does many more things and gets involved in many more teaching behaviors. This, in turn, tends to make the critique session more diffused and apparently less effective.

Another feature of this short micro-lesson is that it allows for more frequent practice by the teacher. Instead of having one long training period followed by a long critique, the microteaching clinic proceeds on the premise that many short teaching periods followed immediately by critique periods can bring about more desirable results.

Finally, for pre-service teachers the micro-lesson is one link in a progressive chain to actual classroom teaching. The next link is the micro-class.

The micro-class

Micro-classes usually come after a few weeks of short micro-lessons, and after the trainee has acquired a base of teaching skills. The micro-lesson pattern is not completely dropped at this point, however. Throughout the weeks devoted primarily to the micro-class, short micro-lessons are scheduled. The micro-class pattern is loosely based on the idea of team teaching. Three or four trainees of the same discipline are grouped together to design and teach a unit of instruction in their subject field. Each lesson is from 20 to 25 minutes in length and the unit comprises a series of 12 lessons. Since continuity is important, the group teaches the same four or five students each day. Also, while the micro-classes are going on, all the trainees receive instruction in new skills. Usually, the skills worked on during the micro-class pattern are skills more appropriate to longer lessons. During their longer micro-classes the trainees are expected to demonstrate not only these new skills, but also the earlier-acquired ones.

A week before the micro-classes begin, a group of trainees is formed and meets on two or three occasions. First they decide what they will teach, and then decide how and who will teach. A micro-class session takes a full hour: approximately 20 minutes of teaching and 30 minutes of group critique. After the teacher for that day has spent 20 to 25 minutes teaching, general feedback forms, and also rating forms on the skill being worked on, are handed out to the students. After the students complete the forms, they leave the room and the group critique begins, with primary attention usually being given to the skill under investigation. After this, the group moves quickly on to other concerns. Were the objectives of the lesson clear to the student? Was the transition from yesterday's to today's lesson clear? How could the lesson have been improved? How could the teacher's presentation have been improved? Are there any changes suggested in the lesson plan for tomorrow, or changes in strategy for the entire unit? Also, if the lessons have been videotaped, supervisor and trainees identify critical incidents during the lesson's review.

An important part of the supervisor's role in the micro-lesson is ensuring that the critique periods have a constructive tone. Negative criticism by peers can be quite upsetting to some. It is important, therefore, that the supervisor be a model of constructive criticism and that he keep the critique sessions from becoming overly threatening to individual trainees.

The micro-class has its own special advantages. For one thing, it extends the skilled training dimension of microteaching. During the longer micro-classes the trainee is supposed to continue practicing the skills learned earlier. He has a chance to knit together the performance of several skills. Also, he tries out new skills. However, during the micro-class pattern the attention of the group is drawn to many other issues besides teaching skills. The content dimension becomes much more important. The various teaching strategies are discussed. Trainees are particularly responsive to the opportunity to deal with a longer unit. For the first time they come in contact with the task of laying out a large block of work and considering all aspects, from behavioral objectives to methods of evaluating learning. During the micro-class they see the skeletal and structural objectives take on flesh and blood before their students. They begin to grapple with new problems, such as transitions within lessons and transitions from lesson to lesson.

Another benefit is that the trainees learn to work in groups. They seem to enjoy the stimulation of many minds working on the same problem. Most of them enjoy the chance to see their colleagues teach. Many discover that they are not the only ones with problems. Normally, they are quite interested in how another trainee goes about teaching a lesson, since each has been involved in the planning and has usually visualized how he would go about teaching it.

In general, there are two assets to this team-teaching approach in microteaching. First, the trainees develop an openness about their teaching. They see the value of feedback and criticism from their colleagues. They see how they can help and be helped. Second, they become increasingly realistic about their own teaching. Seeing other beginners helps them appreciate their own instructional strengths and weaknesses.

Research clinical sessions

The third pattern used in the Stanford Microteaching Clinic is research clinical sessions. Here the purpose is to extend our knowledge of teaching skills and various training protocols to bring about a high performance of these skills. Each summer, in order to answer the growing number of questions provoked by microteaching, several days are set aside for research clinical sessions.

The distinguishing feature of the research clinical sessions is that they are self-contained units. Each trainee is instructed and given the chance to practice in a single block of time, usually between two and three hours in length. The research clinical sessions are self-contained so that training in the teaching skills can be conducted under rather strict experimental conditions. This pattern allows for control over instructional variables, and over practice and feedback variables. The fact that training occurs during one concentrated period of time lessens the possibility of contamination. The trainees have little opportunity to interact with one another. The time between instruction and practice is the same for all trainees, or is purposely manipulated for experimental reasons.

Recently the research-clinic pattern has been used extensively in modeling experiments. A taped model of a particular teaching skill becomes the primary unit of instruction. A description of the basic step in this self-contained training pattern should illuminate the procedure. The trainee comes to the clinic having prepared a 5-minute lesson. First he teaches the lesson without having received specific instructions. This lesson is taped and is used as a diagnostic base for the experiment. The trainee then views the model tape, with the intention of incorporating the demonstrated skill in his following practice sessions. After he has seen the model tape, he sees the tape of his initial performance. This is followed by a reteach session in which he practices the modeled skill. The cycle of practice, the trainee's viewing the model, and his own performance is continued until the final step when the trainee reviews his own performance for the last time. The exact sequencing of these events and the numbers of practice sessions and exposures to the model are varied according to the complexity of the skill and the research questions under consideration.

The research clinical sessions are seen as an essential part of the microteaching operation. Building a number of these sessions into the clinic's summer schedule allows us to systematically test questions that have arisen and to extend our knowledge of teaching skills and the capabilities and limitations of microteaching.

3-4 THE SUPERVISOR

The microteaching supervisor is essentially a teacher. His role is to increase and refine performance of the skills that serve as the objectives of the clinic. His responsibility is twofold: He must help the trainee develop the ability to perform a skill and he must also help him understand when the skill should be applied. His dual role parallels the technical skills of teaching and professional decisions dimensions of the clinic. With regard to the first of these roles, the supervisor aids the trainee in the discrimination of the skill and reinforces his performance of it. He helps the trainee to understand the behaviors that constitute the skill and to become sensitive to the cues that signal when the skill should be performed. When the trainee performs the skill, or begins to approximate the performance of it, the supervisor reinforces his behavior. In other words, the supervisor helps the trainee see what he should do, and tells him when he has done it.

The second part of the supervisor's role relates to the application of the skills. Having a repertory of reinforcement skills does not ensure good classroom application. Good performance depends on when and where the skills are used. The supervisor, then, must aid the trainee in making these professional decisions.

In the Stanford Microteaching Clinic, supervisors are teaching and research assistants who normally have had a minimum of three years of classroom experience. They work as supervisors while pursuing higher degrees in education. Each supervisor is assigned between eight and ten teacher trainees at the start of the summer, and he works with this group for a year. After a summer of microteaching, the supervisor visits his trainees out in the schools and, among other things, he follows up on the skills training they received in the clinic. During the summer and throughout the year the supervisor devotes 20 hours a week to the training program. Although the supervisors are paid, most see it as important experience that directly contributes to their own future goals. Very few of the supervisors, however, have had previous training as supervisors. Therefore special attention must be given to this need.

The supervisor (here serving also as videotape operator) takes notes during the microteaching lesson and uses the video recording selectively. He rarely uses the entire recording during the critique session.

The training of supervisors is greatly simplified in a micro-setting. This is due to the high specificity of the clinic's aims. When someone joins the supervisory staff, he does not need a great deal of skill before he can work with trainees. In a sense, all that he needs in the beginning is to stay one chapter ahead of the trainee.

New supervisors go through a 30-hour course, spread out over the summer, that deals with four interrelated issues: First, the component-skills approach to teaching is explained and discussed. Second, the rationale and benefits of focusing on discrete skills is explored. Third, the various strategies and techniques of supervision are explained. Fourth, the individual teaching skills and related professional decisions that make up the curriculum of the microteaching clinic are examined.

New supervisors receive instruction in the techniques and strategies of supervision. Several approaches to supervising teachers—such as reinforcement techniques and indirect and nondirect supervision—are demonstrated. The ongoing microteaching clinic is used as a laboratory and each new supervisor is expected to practice these approaches. Tapes of their critique session with the trainees are made, and are used as the bases for group discussion. Also, model tapes of both good and bad supervisory techniques are used as a stimulus for examining the problems inherent in the supervisory process. The model tapes are effective in teaching skills of supervision in the same way that they are helpful in teaching skills of instruction. The component behaviors are highlighted and clarified. The models of poor supervisory technique appear to be particularly helpful in exposing potential weaknesses. Frequently, a brief tape of a clumsy, punishing supervisory session is more effective in helping people change their approach than long hours of discussion and explanation. To twist a Chinese proverb, "One tape is worth more than a thousand words."

The training session for supervisors is also used by supervisors to discuss their individual problems. For instance, a supervisor who is having trouble getting one of his trainees to stop talking and to question students more presents the problem to the group. One way he does this is to provide some of the background on the trainee and then show the group a few tapes of micro-lessons. Once the problem is clarified and the supervisor has stated what efforts he has taken to remedy the difficulty, the group suggests approaches. Several alternatives usually come out of the session, alternatives which the supervisor can try out. Such sessions not only show each supervisor that there is a variety of approaches to any one problem, but they show each that his problems are not unique. This approach appears to have the added advantage of solidifying the supervisory group and establishing a common dialog among them that lasts long after their training sessions are over.

3-5 MICROTEACHING STUDENTS

Fundamental to the microteaching concept is the conviction that microteaching is *real* teaching. Whether microteaching is engaged in by a neophyte or a gnarled veteran, its intention is to provide a practice setting for teaching. Students, therefore, are as basic to the microteaching clinic as trainees. The microteaching students provide the realism in this teaching encounter. The students are a crucial variable in the clinic's operation. Thus special attention needs to be given to the recruitment, selection, and training of students.

Recruitment of microteaching students

Most students really enjoy being part of a microteaching clinic. They take their responsibility seriously, work very hard, and are willing and thoughtful in the use of the evaluation instruments. Perhaps the reason they do so well is that they are highly flattered that someone is relying on them to improve the process of teaching and learning.

In most locations the recruitment of students for the clinic presents no problem. This is particularly true when clinics are used for in-service training in public schools. The most direct means for recruiting students in a school is to ask for volunteers. Most schools have service groups that can be called on to provide microteaching students. For example, involvement in a microteaching clinic would be a very valuable activity for the Future Teachers of America.

Recruiting microteaching students for a clinic to be held outside a school setting is a different matter, but hardly a major obstacle. Much of what we shall discuss here applies mainly to situations such as one finds in institutions that have teacher education programs but that do not have a ready supply of high school students from which to draw.

Work in a microteaching clinic is a very exciting job for students. A minimum of publicity has inevitably brought a plethora of applicants. The idea of being paid to go to school has great appeal to many students. Experience has shown, however, that two points in particular should be clarified for applicants. *First:* The clinic's purpose is the training of teachers rather than the training of students. Although microteaching students will receive interesting and, it is hoped, valuable instruction, this is a by-product of their involvement in the clinic. Their work in the clinic will not provide them with remediation for their special problems. Nor is the clinic established as an enrichment school. They are there to perform a training service. *Second:* Being a microteaching student is primarily a job, a job for which they are paid. The microteaching students in the Stanford clinic were paid $1.00 an hour. In return, the students are expected to take on certain responsibilities. An applicant should realize from the outset that if he is irresponsible or becomes a nuisance, he will be replaced by another student. The microteaching clinic does not have the facilities to cope with behavior problems or chronic absenteeism. Both these points—the purpose of the clinic and the fact that it is a job—should be brought home to the applicants.

Selection of students

The actual choice of students for work in the clinic should be dictated by the purposes of the clinic. If the clinic's purpose is to train teachers for certain types of schools, the microteaching students should be similar to students found in those schools. For instance, if the clinic is designed to train teachers for inner-city schools, microteaching students should be typical of the students in the target schools. In a recent Peace Corps clinic at Stanford, for example, the trainees were going to be teaching in a Philippine elementary school; therefore the students were Filipino.

The number of microteaching students selected depends on the specifications and structural conditions of the clinic. Once these are clear, it is a simple matter to determine how many students will be needed. There are two major considerations in the selection of microteaching students.

First: The microteaching students should be representative of those the trainees will contact in the schools. For the first two microteaching clinics at Stanford, we didn't especially try to obtain a representative sample of students. We simply took the easy way out, and employed the children of faculty members, who tended to be a very bright and intellectually aggressive group. In subsequent summers, we took greater care in the selection of students. When we advertised the positions, we made it known that all students were equally eligible. The applications asked for descriptive data that made it simple to determine the achievement level of the applicants. From these applications we chose a bell-shaped curve of students at varying achievement levels. This procedure ensured an approximation of a representative group.

Portability of the videotape equipment is an important consideration. Depending on the variety and location of clinic stations, ease of transport may outweigh the convenience of operating equipment which is less mobile. When permanent clinics are established, it becomes convenient to have fixed installations.

Second: The grade level of the microteaching students is a relevant factor. One must keep in mind the age group the trainees will teach. The trainees in the Stanford clinic were preparing for secondary teaching. Since they were to teach in grades seven through twelve, with a large number teaching in the tenth and eleventh grades, the selection of students reflected these considerations.

Training of microteaching students
There are two types of training for microteaching students. The first is *initial training,* before they work in the clinic. The second is *main-*

Student raters criticize lesson presentation generally or with respect to specific skills. Trainee teachers may receive such feedback orally, in writing, or both. Microteaching student teams are assigned to a lounge area, with informal supervision, so that they can relax between teaching sessions. Supervision of this area is informal. Students typically have every fifth clinic teaching module for rest.

tenance training, given at intervals during the clinic's operation. The initial training can be completed during a morning, a week or so before the beginning of the clinic. Much of the initial training involves clarification of the students' role in the clinic. First we tell the students the overall intentions of the clinic. We stress the fact that the clinic is not a school, but a training program for future teachers. We make it clear to the students that they are there to perform a service, and that therefore we cannot tolerate any discipline problems. We explain the importance of showing up on time and keeping to schedules. Second, after we have given the students an overview of the clinic and the do's and don't's of their work, we talk about the feedback dimension of their assignment. We give them rating forms and explain the various items. Once this is clear, we show them several tapes of sample lessons taught by beginning teachers. After each tape, they are instructed to rate the teacher's performance, using the form. We quickly tabulate their ratings. When there is wide disagreement on particular items, we ask students at the extremes to state the evidence they used for their ratings. The intention here is not to force them toward consensus in rating, but to sensitize them to some of the competing interpretations of specific teaching performances. Other than this discussion, there is no pressure brought to bear on the students to bring about agreement. If microteaching is to be a real teaching situation, it is essential that students feed back to the trainees their own perceptions. Their raw perceptions may vary widely, but this seems more sensible than programming the students to feed back predigested judgments. The initial training phase, then, tells microteaching students what to expect, and gives them practice in rating teaching performance. This first phase of training takes about three hours.

The microteaching students also receive training periodically after the clinic is in operation. Since each teaching skill has its own rating-feedback form, microteaching students need to be trained to use these forms. This training consists of giving the microteaching students a clear idea of the skill and an understanding of the terminology in each item of the feedback form. The skill is explained through demonstrations and discussion. After they have an idea of what they will be rating, each item on the form is gone over to clarify the terminology and behavioral referents. Other training meetings are called all during the time the clinic is operating. Normally, these meetings deal with issues like adherence to the schedule and various mechanical problems.

In a clinic the size of Stanford's, one has to have a microteaching student coordinator. This person's job is to coordinate the activities of the students, making sure they all receive adequate training, reshuffling teams of students when necessary, and generally supervising the work of the students. In brief, the microteaching student coordinator deals with the students' problems and tries to make the most effective use of their services. On the rare occasion when a microteaching student has to be dismissed, this action is initiated and carried through by the coordinator.

Quite often the microteaching students can be a valuable source of information or feedback on the operation of the clinic itself. They are so enmeshed in the workings of the clinic that frequently they can see things others cannot. They can identify such things as wasted time in the schedule and ambiguous terminology in the rating forms. Although the microteaching student coordinator usually acts as an intermediary for this information, it helps to hold a conference of the microteaching students at the end of a clinic's operation, simply to tap their thoughts about how the operation of the clinic can be made more efficient. Also, issues relating directly to them—such as scheduling, payment, and their role as feedback agents—can be given thorough attention.

One of the unresearched issues related to microteaching is the effect of the experience on the microteaching students. Informal, impressionistic data have been gathered from the microteaching students, their parents, and counselors. Most of these data are encouraging. Microteaching students enjoy the experience and are particularly taken by the idea of being paid to learn. One other source of evidence for this is the fact that most of them apply to be microteaching students the following year. However, we have tended to move away from the policy of rehiring students, since we value freshness of perceptions more than sophistication. Several counselors and teachers have told us that the microteaching experience has had a very beneficial effect on student attitudes. When they get back to school in September they are much more interested in their work and much more sympathetic to the aims of the school.

One of the rather amusing effects of the microteaching students' summer experience is that they become quite critical of the teaching process. During the clinic it is common to see students arguing among themselves right after a class about the effectiveness of a trainee's use of nonverbal cues or inquiry technique. Occasionally during the school year the microteaching students will see clinic staff members in their schools and give them an analysis of their teachers' performance: "And Mr. Roland only knows half of the reinforcement skills—the negative half." One of the interesting questions that should be examined is the effect of the experience on the career choice of the microteaching student.

Two girls who had spent the summer working together had opposite reactions. One said that before the microteaching clinic she was convinced she wanted to be a teacher. After criticizing teaching all summer, she felt that teaching "just didn't seem like fun any more." For her friend, the story was reversed. She had never thought teaching was very challenging or exciting. A summer in the clinic convinced her that she had to become a teacher. "I never thought there was so much involved in good teaching." Although several have indicated that they have decided to become teachers, there is still some time before this stated desire will be put to the test.

3-6 VIDEOTAPE RECORDING

As stated earlier, videotaping is not an essential part of the microteaching process. In many places microteaching has been carried out successfully without the use of this equipment. Videotape recording is a frill. However, it is a frill that can substantially further the aims of microteaching. Videotaping strengthens the microteaching process in two ways: *First,* it is excellent for both the development and display of models of the various teaching skills. Although this modeling function may soon be performed by 16mm or 8mm films, in the present developmental stage the videotape recorder serves well. *Second,* the videotape recorder is a powerful feedback source in the microteaching process. It helps the trainee understand his own performance and also serves as a teaching tool for the supervisor. This second function of the videotape recorder—as feedback instrument—is the function we shall discuss in the remainder of this section.

The trainees

Initially, many trainees are understandably nervous about the prospect of having their micro-lessons videotaped. However, this initial hesitance wears away quickly once they discover its benefits for them. Also, the fact that the videotape recorder used in microteaching is not the large studio variety, but the newer, portable unit makes it much less imposing. A microphone is set up between the teacher and the students. In the rear of the room (although this positioning is not the only one possible) the small camera and recorder are stationed. Since the recorders operate quite effectively with the normal illumination available in a classroom, no special equipment is necessary. The compactness of the portable videotape recorder and the lack of a great deal of bulky ancillary equipment mitigates the initial uneasiness of the trainees. Also, the knowledge that tapes are erasable and that their performance will not permanently haunt them eases the minds of many trainees.

After their performances have been taped, many trainees, viewing themselves for the first time, have initial reactions that we call the "cosmetic effect." This is a general term for an overly self-conscious reaction to the first or second tapes. For most trainees, this is the first time they have seen and heard themselves in this manner. It is quite natural that their preoccupations are personal rather than professional. The "cosmetic effect" refers to their concern about coiffure, personal mannerisms (pulling on an ear or not looking directly at students), and anatomical anomalies (overly padded hips, retreating hairlines, skinny legs). Although T. S. Eliot claimed that "human kind cannot bear very much reality," our experience indicates that these personal concerns about physical appearance are short-lived. However, since the trainee displays this concern or curiosity during his first chance to view himself on tape, it seems best not to attempt too much in the way of instruction. Because of this, and because of the candidate's general uncertainty about his first teaching performance, we have tentatively adopted the following policy: During the critique period of initial microteaching sessions the supervisor's role is to allow the trainee to see the full tape and point out only the favorable aspects of the lesson.

Supervisors

While videotapes can extend the competence of supervisors, this does not come about automatically. Most supervisors have to learn how to use it effectively. They have to learn how to combine their supervisory instruction with this new training resource. Without training, supervisors tend to over- or under-use the videotape recorder. When a supervisor over-uses it, he shows a trainee an entire tape, making few if any references to what they are both watching. In this case the supervisor usually expects that the trainee is seeing the same strengths and weaknesses he does. When the supervisor under-uses a tape, he shows only parts of it, and focuses his supervision on entirely different aspects of the teaching performance. It is not uncommon for a beginning supervisor to feel somewhat guilty if he doesn't use the videotape in some way, even though it has no connection with the point he is trying to get across to the trainee. Another common problem is excessive talking while viewing a tape. Frequently new supervisors carry on an impassioned monolog while the trainee is watching the tape of his teaching. In this situation the trainee naturally gets little from either the monolog or the tape.

The major point here is that supervisors should use the tape recording to support and reinforce their supervisory instruction. Not all of a tape has to be shown. Those parts that *are* shown should be chosen to complement the supervisor's aims. The supervisor is trying to get a trainee to become aware of a particular behavior, such as asking students probing questions to support their statements. It makes much more sense for the supervisor to go over critical incidents two or three times than just to view the whole tape once. Another use is for the supervisor to pick a sample of behavior from the tape and have the trainee diagnose either what was right or wrong or questionable about his behavior. Once the trainee has diagnosed his behavior, he is ready to reflect on some of the alternatives which were open to him. In other words, the videotape should not be used by the supervisor in a "show and tell" game, i.e., show him the tape and tell him what he did wrong. The videotape recorder has the great advantage of reproducing the teaching incident. As near as is humanly possible, it can place the supervisor and the trainee in a common frame of reference by objectively reproducing a sample of teaching. Once the supervisor and the trainee share the same understanding, they are at the threshold of great progress.

However, there are the occasional problems. One summer, one of our interns became so completely distraught at the idea of microteaching that at first we thought we would have to completely withdraw her from the clinic. However, an understanding supervisor suggested that perhaps she could teach some students without the videotape and on her own without a supervisor present. So she taught a few lessons to small classes without a supervisor present and without any evaluation. After about two weeks she requested the videotape and the supervisor, and by the end of the summer was participating in the clinic normally.

Videotape operators

Although the videotape recorder is a complex piece of electronic equipment, it is quite simple to operate. Normally a person can be trained to be a videotape operator within an hour or two. No special knowledge, no knowledge of underlying principles, is needed. All that is necessary is (1) the ability to follow basic instructions, and (2) some practice.

In the Stanford microteaching clinic, graduate and undergraduate students were employed as videotape operators at two dollars per hour. One of the most successful and creative operators, however, was an eighth-grade boy who became fascinated with the instrument and was continually seeking new ways to use it. There is no reason to believe that younger children, say even fifth or sixth graders, could not be responsible videotape operators. There is nothing intrinsic to the recorder's operation that requires special manual or intellectual skills.

The daily care and maintenance of a videotape system is no special problem, although certain routines should be established and carefully followed. Also, procedures should be established for the labeling and filing of tapes and tape segments. The major qualification of a good videotape operator is that he be alert to what is happening during the

Even elementary students can be taught to operate simple videotape equipment. Here a student operator checks recording quality after a lesson.

Student cameramen may be used to hold the camera.

Or a fixed camera may be preset in a reasonable range.

micro-lesson. He is usually on his own to follow the general flow of a lesson, although occasionally either the supervisor or the trainee will instruct him to focus on particular students or certain aspects of the lesson. It is important that he be alert to the situation, so that he knows when a close-up of a puzzled student or a wide-angle shot of the whole group would be most helpful. Finally, it is important that the operator and his recorder in no way interfere with the microteaching process. An operator who is loud and boisterous, or who is excessively clumsy and inept, will make his presence known. When he does, he can be a distraction, particularly to the teacher. In a way, good videotape operators are like fine waiters: they are so skillful that one is unaware of their presence.

3-7 SUMMARY

These, then, are the elements of microteaching, as practiced at Stanford University. Institutions with smaller operations should be able to develop a clinic with much less attention to detail than that described here; institutions with large operations may need a much more systematic approach than that described here. In designing and developing a microteaching clinic, however, it is important not to lose perspective. The essential features of microteaching should not be lost in a vain pursuit of the perfectly organized, "pure" microteaching clinic that never was and never will be. The essential feature—providing teachers with a practice setting to work on their professional skills—should be preserved. Just as there are no perfect classrooms, there can be no perfect microteaching clinics.

Chapter 4
Microteaching and the
Pre-Service Training of Teachers

Preparing beginners for their initial teaching experience—whether it be student teaching or internship—has been one of the major soft spots in professional education. Typically, there have been few, if any, bridges between the formal study of education and initial classroom practice. Beginners have been exposed to a series of education courses, and then immersed in an ongoing classroom.

Many teacher education programs, however, have developed extensive programs of classroom observation. Here the beginner normally goes out to schools and observes skillful teachers. Although a sound observation program has many strengths, it has some severe limitations, too.

First: Observation is essentially a passive exercise. The beginner simply watches another teacher performing, and he may be watching with very unsophisticated eyes. If he does learn something, he has little immediate opportunity to practice what he has learned.

Second: The principle behind observation is learning by imitation. Although learning by imitation may have real value in teacher education, it has been very loosely applied in most observation programs. Will the teacher imitate the right things? If the teacher being observed is a good teacher (and this is difficult to determine), will the observer tend to imitate the skills, strategies, and techniques? Or will he tend to imitate a particular style unique to the teacher?

Third: Observation can be very time-consuming, even when the observed classroom is near at hand, as in the case of a university laboratory school. The observer has to spend a good deal of time in the classroom. In a high school the observer must usually stay for a full 50 minutes; in an elementary classroom, perhaps even longer. And still there is no guarantee that what the observer sees will be valuable to him.

What is needed is a method of bridging the gap between instruction in education and classroom practice; a method that combines the energies of beginning teachers, supervisors, and professors of education. Such a method should provide the beginner with real practice in teaching and with training in specific teaching skills and strategies. Microteaching fulfills these functions.

4-1 THE BEGINNING TEACHER

For many new teachers who are thrust into the classroom, the initial teaching experience is a disappointment, if not a disaster. Myriad problems that they only vaguely anticipated become searing realities. They did not realize that teaching would be so complex. They had not anticipated that they would have to be doing so many things at once. They have a hard time finding the proper level of communication to use with students. They have difficulty planning, and, further, they have difficulty translating their carefully worked out plans into classroom activities. They have trouble figuring out how they should act with students who are sometimes just four and five years younger than they. When things go right, they do not know why they are right, and when things go wrong—particularly when they go wrong—they do not know why they do. Even if they do learn by their mistakes during their initial months in the classroom, their students often have elephantine memories and will not let them forget their mistakes. Their students have "typed," "psyched," and "sorted" them. Microteaching can help the beginner avoid many of these initial problems.

The problem of the complexity of the classroom is one that is not often appreciated by pre-service teachers. By the time they have graduated from college, most of them have sat in classrooms watching teachers for approximately 14,000 hours. Although one would expect those who plan to teach, especially, to have an appreciation of the complex act of bringing several human beings to an understanding of certain principles or information, this does not seem to be the case. One reason might be that as students they sit in class and carry on a mental—and only occasionally a verbal—dialog with their teacher. They analyze or simply observe teaching from the point of view of the receiver. They have been trying to understand and to learn from their teacher. When they reverse roles and begin teaching, however, they are faced with an entirely new set of problems. As teachers they often act as transmitters of ideas or guiders of a dialog. When they do they have to deal with many minds at one time. Frequently, they are trying to bring many people simultaneously to an understanding of the material they are teaching. The real practice in teaching that microteaching provides enables the beginner to get a feel for the complexity of teaching in a simplified context. Although he may be teaching only a handful of students, he has to engage in this dialog with all of them at the same time. As one first-year teacher put it, "I never realized it, but teaching is like conducting an orchestra. You have to lead a whole group of people from the start of an idea to the end. As conductor, you are to bring everyone into the act, at least mentally. That's much harder than I imagined. When I was a student, and being 'conducted,' I was like a soloist. I just had to pay attention to the conductor and take care of my own performance."

In the microteaching clinic the teacher is forced to deal with the problem of developing an idea with several people simultaneously. However, since he is teaching only three or four students, the problem is not nearly as overwhelming as it is in a regular classroom. Normally, he teaches content of his own choosing, and he must orchestrate so that all the students learn. In this regard one of the common mistakes of all beginning teachers is to focus on the responsive students and ignore the unresponsive ones. In his enthusiasm his attention gravitates to the most receptive students and he paces his lesson according to the cues received from these students. This phenomenon happens even in the reduced setting of microteaching, but here there is an opportunity to correct it. In the lesson critique that follows, the supervisor can point this out to the beginner, using both his own observations and feedback from students. When videotapes are available, the supervisor can replay a tape and show the teacher how he began teaching all of the students and soon shifted to teaching just one or two. In subsequent micro-lessons, this problem, now that it has been exposed, can be dealt with and solved.

One of the unanticipated problems which many new teachers face is finding an appropriate level of communication for their students. As college students or graduates, they often have highly developed vocabularies and can handle ideas quickly and efficiently. Their normal explanation of ideas and their description of events can seem like shorthand to their students. Some teachers, therefore, tend to rush too quickly over concepts because of a reliance on unduly symbolic language and a paucity of examples. Others, excessively sensitive to this problem, oversimplify and talk down to their students. There are few things that annoy students more than this. How often have we heard students complain, "She talks to us as if we were babies." However, it is expecting a great deal of a beginning teacher to immediately find an appropriate level of communication for third graders or high school sophomores, as the case may be. In the microteaching clinic, candidates not only instruct students of the same age and grade as they will instruct during their initial teaching in the schools, but also students of a variety of ages. For many this experience of teaching students of different ages helps them decide at which grade level they would like to teach. In effect, then, the microteaching clinic allows the beginner to experiment and discover the appropriate vocabulary and pacing for the presentation of ideas. The several feedback dimensions are particularly helpful to the beginner in finding a suitable style and language level.

Beginning teachers, as they enter the profession, are asked to make a rather dramatic role change. For many this presents no problem. However, there are those who tend toward the extremes of either rigid formality or loose informality. The errors and fumblings that a new teacher makes in groping for a correct social distance can harry him during his entire first year. The microteaching clinic, since it is a real teaching situation, allows the beginner to adjust to his new role as teacher and acquire a comfortable and suitable social distance. He can make his mistakes in a "safe" environment. The case of one young woman who was determined not to become an aloof teacherish type illustrates this point. She showed up for her microteaching appointment well prepared to teach a short lesson. However, she was rushed for lunch and did not see why she could not eat an apple while she was instructing. Although she taught her lesson reasonably well and demonstrated the skill that was to be learned, she received a great shock when her supervisor showed her the student responses to her lesson. The students were indignant that she would do such a thing! They felt that she was being disrespectful to them by eating an apple in front of them and was acting totally "unteacherish." Apparently they were quite distracted by her innocent apple and paid little attention to her lesson. This particular beginner became vividly aware of the very conservative nature of students and of how innocuous actions can have unanticipated effects on learning. The point here is not that microteaching imposes an orthodox model of teaching on the beginner, but it exposes him to the ground rules of the classroom culture. If he wishes to depart from these unwritten rules, he at least knows what to expect and what the price will be.

A major advantage of the microteaching clinic for the beginning teacher is that it equips him with an array of teaching skills before he assumes instructional responsibility in a school. In each microteaching lesson the beginner is not only trying to instruct in some aspect of his discipline, but also to practice a specific training skill. A basic premise of the microteaching clinic is that there are specific teaching skills and that some of these can be developed in a constructive teaching situation. Some of the target skills in past clinics have been the various questioning techniques, reinforcement, student participation, initial set induction techniques, classroom control techniques and various presenting skills, such as explaining and illustrating.

The purpose of this training, we repeat, is to enable the beginner to develop proficiency *before* he enters the classroom. The microteaching clinic does not pretend to equip the beginner for all the skills of teaching. For one thing, they have not all been identified and perhaps never will be. The intention is to give the beginner facility with several key skills and to give him understanding of how and when they can be most suitably applied. After he is in the classroom, the graduate of the microteaching clinic does not perform like a training rat demonstrating his skill at running various mazes. Nor does microteaching, as Bernard

McKenna of San Francisco State College suggests, freeze the beginning teacher's style by forcing him to be imitative.[1] Rather he is a free agent, with the added confidence that he has many teaching skills on which he can draw when he needs them. Instead of learning these skills by trial and error in his class, he spends his time perfecting these skills and acquiring new ones.

4-2 SUPERVISORS

One of the unforeseen but major benefits of the microteaching clinic is that it helps make supervision much more potent. Having the supervisor and his beginning teachers work together through many lessons before the beginners have their first in-school experiences strengthens supervision considerably. The overall benefit is that the supervisor knows his teachers, knows their strengths and weaknesses, knows how to talk to them and what to expect from them. For the beginning teachers the presence of a supervisor is as integral to a microteaching lesson as the students. Beginners in the microteaching training therefore become quite accustomed, right from the start, to being observed by and having conferences with supervisors. As a result, when they are supervised in the schools, the whole process is a familiar one to them. The new teacher is accustomed to discussing his teaching from a critical viewpoint. He is familiar with the pattern of searching with the supervisor for alternative ways of teaching content, and of standing back and objectively assessing his practice. He is confident that supervision can and will make a difference in his teaching. Just as a supervisor knows what to expect from a teacher, the teacher knows what to expect from a supervisor. This seems to make supervision much less threatening to the beginner and not as emotionally charged as is frequently the case.

Since the microteaching clinic is a low-pressure, practice environment, the supervisor can more easily make the trainee aware of distracting idiosyncrasies. Such gross problems as not looking at students, speaking in a voice that is too high or too shrill or too fast, standing rigidly at a lectern, or casually tugging at a girdle—all these things can be dealt with. The problems that can be almost playfully handled in a microteaching clinic can be ego-shattering for a teacher if they are not attacked until he is in the school.

Certainly one of the most critical periods in a teacher's career is the very first weeks of teaching. This is the period when he is most plastic. This is, also, the period when the students test him and when he is most vulnerable. And this is the period when a supervisor can either give maximum help or become just another frustrating irrelevancy. It seems obvious that the supervisor who has worked through the microteaching clinic with his teachers is in a much more powerful position than the supervisor who enters the picture only at this critical period. When supervision begins during the first weeks of teaching, the teacher not only must learn a whole new role, but must also establish a new relationship with a supervisor at the same time.

Ideally—perhaps even probably—the experience and training gained by being a microteaching supervisor transfers its good effects to regular supervisory duties. What evidence we have confirms the following statement by an experienced supervisor: "Microteaching has given me a whole new perspective on supervision. I've carried the microteaching approach to supervision into my regular supervisory tasks. For the first time I feel as though I am making progress. I think I'm really helping my teachers. Also, I finally have a sense of what I'm supposed to be doing."

The training of supervisors of beginning teachers is an area that has received little attention in the profession. Frequently, supervisors are recruited on the basis of their teaching skill rather than their ability to help people change their behavior. In large programs where there are many supervisors working with teaching candidates, it is often difficult to train and supervise the supervisors. As we said earlier, the microteaching clinic enables the teacher education program to systematically train and observe the supervisors.

4-3 THE TEACHER EDUCATION PROGRAM

A microteaching clinic can be a unifying, tightening force in a teacher education program. When the clinic is an integral part of the total program, several benefits accrue. First, it brings the faculty together to decide on common objectives for the program. Second, it keeps the faculty and staff in close touch with the actual teaching performances of their students. Third, it enables the program to take a major step toward individualizing the training of teachers. Fourth, it provides both staff and teaching candidates with more realistic evidence regarding the candidates' suitability for teaching. Fifth, it provides the entire program with a valuable research tool.

Frequently teacher education programs have the loftiest of goals, but they are goals that lack any real specificity. Programs hope to turn out good teachers but never decide what good teaching involves and never really communicate this to the candidates. In making up the curriculum for a microteaching clinic, the faculty is forced to decide what they want their teachers to do, what behaviors they want them to possess. Though this can be a difficult and occasionally a painful task for a faculty to engage in, it is a very healthy one. The program decides in part, at least, what it is trying to accomplish. The clinic, then, becomes the link between the program's goals and the candidates' teaching behavior.

In a pre-service teacher education program the microteaching clinic is usually held on campus. This provides professors with an opportunity to see their beginning teachers in action. By observing the teacher candidates for short, concentrated periods in the clinic, professors are able to make the necessary adjustments in their courses to meet their observed needs. Thus they quickly gain an idea of the general competence of their students. This knowledge enables them to make important placement decisions. Also, it keeps the trainees in close contact with their supervisors as they all work toward the improvement of the beginning teachers' competence.

Microteaching is a strong forward step toward individualizing the pre-service training of teachers. The major intent of the clinic is to provide the individual candidate with specific teaching skills and training focused on his unique needs. In nautical terms, the microteaching clinic becomes a shakedown cruise for each future teacher. Many of his instructional problems show up in the clinic, and remediation is possible. If a candidate quickly demonstrates proficiency in the skills he is being trained for, he and the supervisor can concentrate on more sophisticated work. If a candidate is having difficulty mastering skills or demonstrates such problems as extreme nervousness, the program has a way of addressing itself to these problems. The microteaching sessions can be tailored for the individual situation. Special training opportunities can be scheduled. Longer or shorter micro-lessons can be arranged. The number of students can be varied if it seems appropriate. If a supervisor is having difficulty helping a candidate with a particular problem, he can call in another supervisor. If videotape equipment is available, the supervisor can have other supervisors view the tape of the candidate to help find a solution.

In the same vein, the trainee may develop problems during student teaching or internship. Some of these can be remedied through his own analysis or through discussions with supervisors and other teachers. Some problems, however, need something stronger. Problems that are rooted in a lack of skill or in a particular behavior pattern of a teacher may not be eradicated through conversation. Microteaching is quite helpful here. Scheduling special sessions and staging situations in which the teacher can work directly on the problem can be quite beneficial. When a beginner acquires a new skill or eradicates a particular behavior problem in an ongoing class it may be quite embarrassing to him. A practice environment in which the beginner can fail without drastic consequences is a much better setting in which to work on the problem.

Frequently people are placed in student teaching positions or internships with little evidence as to their suitability for teaching. They haven't had a chance to test themselves before they take on the responsibility of instructing a large number of students. A microteaching clinic gives them this chance. While a teacher candidate is working in the clinic it occasionally becomes apparent to him or to a supervisor, or both, that the candidate is not ready for the transition to in-school teaching. Frequently the candidate is the first to realize this and the program is able to delay his entering the school. Further, as a result of a candidate's teaching experience in a microteaching clinic, it sometimes becomes apparent to him that he is just not cut out to be a teacher. When this is the case, it is beneficial both to the individual and the program if the candidate faces the situation. Discovering that he is not a teacher appears to upset the person much less when the discovery comes to him in a practice situation than when it happens in the school. One situation is temporarily disappointing. The other is destructively demoralizing.

Finally, a teacher education program can use the microteaching clinic as a tool for a wide range of research efforts. Since real teaching and real learning go on in a microteaching clinic, whole areas of the teaching-learning process can be experimentally examined. The behavioral effects of education courses and other experiences can be tested. Teaching skills and methods can be trained for in the clinic and their effect followed up in the schools. Research in the area of supervision can be especially facilitated in this highly controllable microteaching situation. Experiments that educators want to try out in the schools can be pilot-tested in the microteaching clinic. New curricula can be tested and evaluated. At a time when the profession is being called on to provide much-needed answers about the education of our young, microteaching provides us with a vehicle by which we can get at some of these answers.

REFERENCE

1. McKenna, Bernard, *Student Impact*, page 39, May-June 1968.

Chapter 5
The In-Service Uses of
Microteaching

5-1 SURVIVAL TRAINING FOR TEACHERS

"Give me a good college graduate, and I'll make a good teacher out of him." This statement, which is not uncommon on the lips of school administrators, is based on more than bravado. Administrators have two reasons for making this assertion. First, there is disappointment, generally speaking, in the professional preparation provided new teachers by teacher training institutions. Many of the pressing realities of life in the classroom are ignored. Second, and perhaps more inalterable, is the realization that only so much can be done by teacher training institutions; a great deal of the professional knowledge needed for successful teaching must be learned on the job. In light of the limited time and resources presently allocated to the pre-service training of teachers, much of their education and development becomes the responsibility of the schools.

Although the inadequacies of pre-service training are recognized by administrators and teachers alike, little formal attention is given to the problem in the schools. A very small percentage of the average teacher's working day is devoted to his own training as a teacher. What we have in the teaching profession, then, is a situation in which there is minimal training before the teacher enters the profession and minimal training after he gets into it.

Although this system is the making of many teachers, once they become working faculty members, it is also the undoing of many. On-the-job training is usually a hit-or-miss affair. It is like the military survival training in which a trainee is dropped off into a swamp armed with a knife and a packet of K-rations, and told to report back to the base in seven days. The trainee's assignment is to stay in this foreign territory and survive. The analogy to initial teaching assignments is disturbingly close. Beginning teachers are assigned to classes (often the most unpleasant), armed with a teacher's manual and a course outline, and told to excel. The marvel is that so many survive. However, it is doubtful that this system allows even the naturally gifted to reach their full potential. Then there is the problem of those who are crippled by this "survival training." If teachers are to reach their full professional potential, in-service training ought to be given much more careful attention, more time, and more money. But time and money alone won't solve the problem. New ideas are needed. Microteaching is one such idea.

As we said in the opening chapter, microteaching's greatest potential is in in-service teacher education. The first and perhaps most obvious reason is that there are more teachers with certificates than teachers in training. Second, under our present arrangements few teachers are fully prepared when they begin their initial teaching. Third, many teachers do not realize what their own instructional weaknesses are until they have actually taught for some time. Fourth, microteaching can be used for much more than simply developing teaching skills and strategies. Many of the unique needs of the school can be served through a microteaching clinic.

5-2 WHO CAN MICROTEACHING HELP?

"Who can microteaching help?" might best be answered by another question: "Who has acquired all the skills of teaching and continually practices them at a high level of competence?" In other words, microteaching can aid all those who have not completely mastered the many component skills of teaching. As will be pointed out later, the fact that all the skills of teaching have not yet been identified does not mean that microteaching has only a limited use. There are, however, several distinct groups of teachers for whom microteaching can be especially beneficial.

Most beginning teachers start their careers with a rather narrow array of teaching skills and techniques. During their early years in the classroom, teachers try to improve what they call their "bag of tricks." They polish their performance of skills and acquire new ones. Every teacher knows, however, that there are undoubtedly some skills which he has not quite mastered and that he will never develop. For example, there is the teacher who begins teaching with a very tentative grasp of the skills of nonverbal communication. When he discovers that he cannot control pupils' behavior by the gestures and facial cues, he resorts to controlling it entirely by words. If words work, he will probably abandon the initial attempts at developing nonverbal cues and get in the habit of relying on controlling statements. Although this may be no tragedy, it may be inefficient and help to make his class a rather noxious place to be. Another example is the teacher who has heard a good deal about the merits of inquiry techniques, but when he tries it out in his own class two or three times, he finds that the students either get too excited or fail to get involved. Normally, he will decide that he is not suited for this technique and will concentrate on a more traditional, and perhaps less imaginative, technique. These beginning teachers would benefit from work in the practice setting of microteaching.

Many schools are changing their instructional programs and formats, moving toward more flexible schedules and more varied patterns of instruction, such as large group and individualized instruction. To keep up with these changes, teachers frequently have to learn new roles. What may have been adequate for one educational setting may be inadequate for another. At present, few schools have developed mechanisms to implement the changes in teacher roles. For example, if a school moves into a team teaching pattern, which allows for more small group discussions, what provisions are made to help the teachers acquire the necessary skills to work well as teachers in this setting? Such a school could use a microteaching clinic to help its teachers acquire the needed skills.

What about the teachers who are considered the most outstanding in a school? Can microteaching benefit them? One would assume that even the outstanding teachers still have room for improvement. They, too, probably reached a performance plateau early in their careers, but they have less incentive to improve. The simple fact of being recognized as outstanding teachers may lessen the drive to improve. Another factor in the lack of continuous growth is that these outstanding teachers, like the others, have had no vehicle for improvement. A microteaching clinic would be a stimulus to further increase their competence.

In the teaching profession today women are in the majority. The current career pattern for many women is to teach for a few years, retreat to the home for several years to raise a family, and later to return to teaching. Present certification regulations allow many women to return to the classroom after an absence of ten to fifteen years with little or nothing in the way of professional refresher courses. Microteaching could perform an especially valuable service for these women returning to the classroom. Besides giving them the feel of teaching again, practice in a clinic could help them develop the newer teaching skills and approaches.

5-3 THE UNIQUE USES OF MICROTEACHING IN THE SCHOOLS

The knowledge explosion is one of the facts of life in the latter third of the twentieth century. The flood of new knowledge, the new interpretations and fresh explanations of old facts, and the growth of entirely new disciplines present staggering tasks to those given the responsibility of educating the young. As yet, public education has not found adequate ways to keep teachers abreast of the knowledge explosion. This problem is so serious that it may call for an entirely new approach to professional training in education.

In any event, the continuous education of teachers must be fostered by new attitudes and new approaches. Microteaching represents one such approach. As new curricula and methodologies are developed, teachers should have a chance to gain mastery over them before they actually try them out in the classroom. As we said above, new scheduling procedures call for new instructional modes. Here, again, opportunities for training are needed. The microteaching clinic can provide such training needs. At present, elementary school teachers are being urged to teach the new math and new reading techniques. Many experienced high school language teachers are unprepared to meet the demands of the audiolingual approach. Science teachers are using curricula that stress problem-solving and inquiry. All these teachers could benefit from concentrated practice with feedback in a microteaching clinic. Teachers, instead of learning these new skills in their own classrooms, ought to have the opportunity to acquire them in a more controlled environment. For one thing, the classroom has limited feedback resources. For another, this learning-by-doing approach may be unfair to the students.

Many schools have adopted the team-teaching approach. Frequently, the teams use special materials. A microteaching clinic can provide a realistic test site for the teams to develop these new materials and test different modes of presentation. While one teacher instructs, the other team members can act as evaluators. This use of microteaching to test materials and techniques is not limited to teaching teams. Under the present framework, if a teacher wishes to try a new approach in a particular lesson, he must wait until the following year to test alternatives to that lesson. In microteaching, the teacher can experiment with several alternatives, with a limited number of students each time and with the opportunity for immediate evaluation and additional trials. For example, suppose that an English teacher in an ordinary school situation decides to introduce a unit on poetry by using the songs of Paul Simon and Art Garfunkel. He has no idea whether it will be effective. If he were in a microteaching situation, he could try out several approaches, such as passing out ditto copies of the verses, using fictitious authors' names, or playing the actual recordings. Following this general approach, he should be able to figure out which method would make for the best classroom presentation. In this manner teachers may experiment with new methods and new content with much more satisfactory timing, and without the risk of defeating the purpose of student learning.

One of the things that researchers, teachers, and critics of the schools alike have noted is the lack of a professional dialog among teachers. Teaching is viewed as largely a private affair between the teacher and his students. In the faculty room the teacher usually speaks in broad generalities about his classes. There is no careful discussion of new curricular concepts or ways to solve specific teaching problems. Faculty room conversations cover the range from foreign affairs to the personalities of administrators. Rarely do professional issues sustain attention. Staff and departmental meetings are all too often concerned primarily with administrative matters and broad policy issues. What a teacher actually does in a classroom is hardly ever a matter for discussion. Microteaching can be a catalytic element for bringing teachers together to discuss professional issues. In a microteaching clinic the teaching-learning act is always in the foreground. When a group of teachers watch a microteaching lesson, whether for purposes of demonstration or practice, they have a common experience to discuss. When they have something tangible to get their teeth into, they don't have any trouble sustaining a professional dialog. A third-grade teacher of 18 years' experience reported on the effect of microteaching on her elementary school teaching peers: "Since we have been microteaching on a regular basis our conversations have changed from sales and the weekend to set induction and reinforcement."

The primary aim of supervision is the improvement of instruction. That is the theory, at least. As practiced in too many schools today, supervision no longer means aid to the teacher; it has degenerated into mere evaluation for tenure. Designated supervisors, be they administrators or department heads, are busy people. Hence, since supervision is quite time-consuming and frequently a very sensitive area to the teacher, it is not given the attention it merits. Also, few people have a chance to receive training in supervisory skills.

Microteaching has opened up a new approach to supervision. In a microteaching clinic supervision can be done in a brief, concentrated way. Supervisors do not have to sit through entire lessons or waste time sitting in the back of a classroom while the teacher is engaged in an activity that does not require supervision. Also, much of the sensitivity is taken out of supervision when it is performed in a microteaching setting. For one thing, microteaching is by design a practice situation. Second, the students are not from the teacher's regular class. Therefore the teacher is not bothered by the students' awareness that the supervisor is present. Third, there is no uncomfortable groping around by the supervisor or teacher about what to discuss. That is decided before the teacher begins the lesson. The supervisor and the teacher have a common topic for discussion from the start. Fourth, as mentioned in an earlier chapter, the training of supervisors is greatly simplified in a microteaching setting.

One of the major methods of providing in-service training for teachers is supplying them with resource personnel, people such as curriculum coordinators and consultants. Normally, the resource personnel are limited to simply talking to the teachers about instructional matters. Although this may be valuable, it could be made even more so. Applying the microteaching approach, the resource person could demonstrate what he is talking about by actually teaching a lesson to a few students. Also, teachers would immediately have the chance to practice what the consultant has been suggesting. If nothing else, the resource person's ideas and approaches would be tried out in a realistic setting.

5-4 WHAT DOES IT TAKE?

To develop an in-service microteaching clinic, the most important asset is the realization among the staff that "all is not perfect." If teachers acknowledge this and are ready to act on it, then they are ready to begin microteaching. Although there are basic principles and suggested procedures for microteaching, necessarily there is variation in application from school to school. Each school has unique personalities, concerns, and problems. Even within a school, different teachers may decide to use microteaching for different purposes. Some may wish to concentrate on teaching skills; others may wish to use the clinic for curriculum development. And, just as there are local needs to be served by microteaching, there are local problems to be overcome when one is establishing and operating a microteaching clinic.

The necessary elements for a microteaching clinic were outlined in Chapter 3. When microteaching is to be used in an in-service situation, however, there are some variations. For one thing, an elementary or high school has few problems of finding adequate numbers of microteaching students. Thus, although a teacher education program normally has to hire students, this may not be necessary in an ongoing school. Many schools have service organizations and this type of direct service to teachers should be very appealing to these groups. As mentioned earlier, the Future Teachers of America would seem a particularly appropriate group to involve in microteaching.

Although the function of a supervisor is integral to the microteaching idea, in an in-service clinic it is not necessary that the role be filled by an experienced supervisor; a relatively untrained one may suffice. The choice as to which depends on the purpose of the clinic and those who are receiving training. For beginning teachers, it may be best to have a trained supervisor. In fact, microteaching may be the best possible setting for most of the supervision given to beginning teachers. If we consider the basic function of supervision—to bring aid to the teacher—then the microteaching clinic seems a logical place for this aid to begin. Many of the problems of embarrassment and self-consciousness that usually accompany in-class supervision are eliminated in the practice setting of microteaching.

For more experienced teachers, a colleague may be the most natural person to fill the role of supervisor. Some teachers may enjoy this experience more and profit from it more if they work in teams, taking turns being teacher and supervisor. Another approach is for several teachers to team up, each specializing in particular skills, and each acting as supervisor for all those who receive training in the skill.

If a videotape recorder is to be used, the problem of getting operators is a very minor one. Most schools have audiovisual clubs or a group of students who take on the responsibility of providing such services. The students can be very easily trained as operators for a microteaching clinic.

5-5 SUMMARY

"In-service training" is a tired phrase for an immensely important task. In the past, teachers have had little opportunity to systematically upgrade their teaching skills. A vehicle to aid teachers in their professional growth has been lacking. Microteaching shows great promise of becoming an important means for continued professional development. It holds a kaleidoscope of opportunities for those who are willing to try it.

People visiting the summer microteaching clinic at Stanford University for the first time are frequently awed by what they see. The clinic's setting is a very attractive modern elementary school building. Replacing the school's regular occupants are some 230 young people, from fresh-faced high school students to bearded doctoral candidates. Everyone seems to know what he is doing. The fact is, each is following a very tight, interlocking schedule. The classrooms in which the microteaching goes on are all well equipped with TV monitors, videotape recorders, and even carpeted floors. For the visitor who has come to Stanford to learn how to establish a microteaching clinic in his school district or teacher training program, the clinic is not only impressive, but often discouraging. He has come to learn how to put a rather simple idea into operation, and what he sees is a rather strange combination of private school and television studio. His initial plan of starting a microteaching clinic in his own setting seems to him about as feasible as holding the Democratic national convention in a one-room school.

This visitor—and perhaps the reader—has missed the point. He cannot see a few striking trees for the dense forest. Stanford has had five years of experience, reflection, redesigning, and general tinkering with its clinic. Today it is a highly developed operation. However, five years ago the clinic took shape in the cellar of a dank basement in a neglected corner of the university. It had no trained personnel. It had no fancy hardware. It had no special budget. There were simply a few professors and graduate students testing a new method of preparing beginners for the role of teacher. The visitor seeing that first microteaching clinic may have grasped the essentials of microteaching more easily. Certainly, we were doing nothing that would discourage him.

The purpose of this chapter, then, is to drive home the fact that microteaching is not just a hothouse plant indigenous to the Stanford teacher education program. Rather it is a training concept for teachers that is adaptable to many different settings. In the summer of 1967 James Cooper of Stanford University surveyed the AACTE-affiliated teacher education institutions, and found that over 100 institutions were using microteaching. Many other Peace Corps and Teacher Corps training centers and school districts were also engaged in microteaching. In this chapter we shall talk about seven of these microteaching clinics.

6-1 MICROTEACHING IN THE
PRE-SERVICE TRAINING OF ELEMENTARY SCHOOL TEACHERS

The first application of the microteaching principle to the training of elementary school teachers was made at San Jose State College, San Jose, California, during the summer of 1965. Like Stanford, San Jose State College used its internship training program to experiment with microteaching. The men responsible for the extension of the micro-teaching idea into elementary teacher training are Warren Kallenbach and Robert J. Ramonda, who are also the directors of the elementary intern training program. The first clinic in the summer of 1965 was a pilot project. The response to the clinic from both staff and interns was so strong and the results so promising that the directors designed a project to test microteaching's efficacy. The experiment was designed to compare the efficacy of two programs: the regular summer program of classroom observation and student teaching and a summer micro-teaching program. There were many similarities between the San Jose State College elementary microteaching clinic and the secondary micro-teaching clinic at Stanford University. Both clinics were established to aid interns in preparing for their full-time teaching jobs. Both used the shorter individual lessons and the group-planned micro-class. In both clinics, the intern teachers taught content of their own choosing. Further, both programs made a point of not giving grades for micro-teaching.

There were differences, however, between the two clinics, the most obvious being the difference in size. The San Jose clinic involved 20 interns and 1 supervisor, while the Stanford clinic involved 100 interns and 20 supervisors. There was less stress at San Jose State College on a pre-set curriculum of teaching skills. The elementary interns worked on the general areas of interaction skills and pupil involvement.

The trainees were all college graduates enrolled in a fifth-year teacher education program. Along with their microteaching experiences they took courses in methods, curriculum, and learning theory during the summer. All 20 were preparing to assume teaching responsibilities within a few months. The one supervisor in the San Jose microteaching clinic was an experienced elementary school teacher who had worked with student teachers for many years. She recruited, as students in the clinic, eight elementary school students from her own class. Since she had taught all eight the previous school year, she was able to provide the trainees with a wealth of background information on the microteaching students.

The clinic operated for the entire summer session. Each intern taught from four to six micro-lessons a week. Each lesson was video-taped and gone over in a critique session with the supervisor. The students and supervisor used a modification of the Stanford Teacher Competency Appraisal Guide as a feedback instrument.

One of the major benefits of the San Jose clinic happened as a serendipity. Because there was only one supervisor and only one video-tape recorder, only one group of four students could be taught at a time. This left four elementary students unsupervised. Since no one else was available, the intern trainees were asked to supervise the children. Two interns were assigned to the clinic each hour. While one taught a group of students, the second supervised the other group of students. The interns benefited greatly from this opportunity to observe and talk with elementary students. The students were on their own and free from the pressures of an instructional situation. The interns were quite grateful for this contact. They felt that they came to know all the students quite well. They discovered their uniqueness, and saw the differences in individual students' classroom and out-of-class behavior. They felt that their unstructured, supervisory experience with the children increased their ability to work with them on a one-to-one basis.

Microteaching in Other Settings

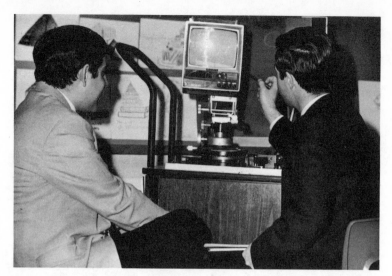

Supervisors are encouraged to limit their critique to one or two specific teaching skills so that a teacher, in the reteach sessions, may focus on improving these skills. This tactic has been very successful in producing immediate and dramatic changes in teaching behavior.

The staff of the clinic can plan a variety of training modes to develop new microteaching alternatives, provide for differences in teachers, or emphasize certain skills. A microteaching setting makes possible more control of the teaching environment.

Like most beginning efforts, the San Jose microteaching clinic was not a flawless success. One difficulty pointed out by the interns was that all the students were fifth graders. Many of the interns were soon to be teaching children in lower grades. They felt that microteaching experiences with younger children would have been more beneficial. Also, since this was one of the earlier microteaching efforts, no models of instructional skills and strategies were available. Another problem related to program morale: Those interns who were not included in the microteaching group felt that they were being cheated. In one week nine of the interns who were randomly assigned to the normal program of observation and student teaching requested to be transferred into the microteaching group.

When Norma Millar, the supervisor, discussed the program, she enumerated several benefits of the clinic. High on her list was the observation that the interns lost their reservations toward students and began perceiving them as individuals. Also, she felt that the attitudes of these beginning teachers toward students was revealed by their work in the clinic. This was particularly true, she felt, in the case of the interns' attitudes toward slow learners. She also noted that the microteaching interns became believers in the value of instructional materials. Although the interns were initially hesitant about bringing realia into class, the fifth graders' response was so favorable that the interns went to very imaginative ends to find materials. They discovered that by using very simple materials, they were able to teach subject matter that was conceptually very sophisticated.

This experiment at San Jose State College which compared the traditional summer program with a microteaching program did not result in any conclusive findings. On the basis of the evaluative instruments used, neither group of interns demonstrated superior teaching in the field. Kallenbach, however, pointed out an important implication for teacher education.

The study demonstrated that elementary intern teaching candidates can be just as effective after a summer Microteaching Program as candidates in a regular summer student teaching program and achieve this objective at a very considerable saving in time for staff and intern candidates.[1]

6-2 MICROTEACHING IN A SCHOOL DISTRICT

The use of microteaching by the teachers and administrators of the Jefferson County school district represents a rather spectacular departure from the typical clinic approach and shows how thoughtful professionals can tailor an innovation to their own desires and needs.

Jefferson County school district is a kindergarten-through-twelfth-grade district in Colorado. The district has undergone tremendous growth in the last 18 years. In 1950 the Jefferson County school district was formed through the unification of 39 districts, then serving a total student population of 11,000. Today the enrollment is 57,000, and climbing at the rate of 3000 new students each year. Currently the district employs more than 2000 teachers working in 120 schools spread out over 790 square miles in suburban Denver. As a result of its growth rate and the normal teacher turnover, the district must hire approximately 500 new teachers each year.

The growth and geographic spread of the Jefferson County school district have caused an acute in-service problem. The constant flow of new, inexperienced teachers into the schools underscored the need for effective in-service training both to develop and sharpen the skills of beginning teachers and to extend their professional competencies. The schools are scattered over such a wide area that there is little opportunity for the faculties of different buildings to work together on such programs. Also, there were few people equipped to take on leadership for in-service training on the individual building level.

To remedy this situation, the district decided to sponsor the Extended Summer Program, which in essence is a teacher training program. This program, started in 1965, runs for seven weeks each summer. It has been worked out with Colorado College at Greeley and participants receive university credit, with tuition being shared by the individual teachers and the school district. The program has morning and afternoon sessions. In the morning there is a summer school program for students, who are divided into groups of 100 and assigned to teams of 12 teachers. Each team of 12 teachers is further broken down into three groups of four. These teams rotate responsibility, one week planning instruction, one week teaching the 100 students, and one week observing the instruction of the group that is teaching. During the afternoon session, when most of the students have left school, the teachers get together in seminars, workshops, and team projects. In the afternoon session the focus of attention is on the teaching that went on in the morning session. Just before starting the Extended Summer Program in 1965, Dr. Dwight Allen introduced microteaching to the teachers and administrators of the Jefferson County schools. Since then it has been a mainstay of their teacher training program and a catalyst for change in the entire district. Although the program has no formal microteaching clinic, with schedules and set curriculum, microteaching is going on all the time. Since everyone is familiar with it, teams and individual teachers "order up" microteaching to their own specifications. The teachers decide which skills to work on, the length of lessons, and the number and grade level of students. In other words, they construct microteaching experiences that help them work on problems they have identified.

The three teams-within-a-team use microteaching in different ways. The four teachers who are planning presentations they will teach the following week construct microteaching sessions to test various approaches to practice strategies and individual skills. Content, too, is tried out in the microteaching setting. Microteaching is the team's reality test, which they use before they instruct the large group of 100 students. Groups of four who are teaching and observing use microteaching to critique and improve the quality of daily instruction. Since the morning sessions are taped, parts of the lesson that need more work are gone over. Microteaching sessions are set up to try out alternatives and to help teachers who are having difficulty with particular skills.

The students used in these afternoon microteaching sessions are drawn from morning summer school. There has been no problem in getting students for the afternoon session. Usually, the parents of these students are invited to sit in and observe the teachers working to improve their professional skills. These parent visitations have apparently been extremely effective in demonstrating to the parents the teachers' concern for good instruction.

Microteaching is not simply fenced into the Extended Summer Program. It is very much a part of the daily life of the district. One of the primary aims of the program is to prepare in the summer a cadre of teacher-leaders who would take charge of in-service programs during the school year. To this end, efforts have been made to get representatives from each building involved in the program. They, in turn, return to their schools in the autumn and work with their colleagues to establish in-service programs. These programs receive district support, but are completely determined by the desires of the local faculties. Microteaching is one of the most popular in-service techniques used during the year, and is being implemented in most of the district's 120 schools. As evidence: At the request of local faculties, the district has acquired more than 60 portable videotape systems in order to support microteaching.

Further, microteaching is credited with stimulating great change in the district and immense growth among teachers. The component-skills-of-teaching concept has taken firm hold among the faculties, and microteaching has supplied the practice setting in which teachers can work on these skills. However, as stated earlier, the Jefferson County teachers are not settling for the tried-and-true. They have taken the basic ideas presented to them three years ago and stretched and shaped them to fit their own purposes. Two examples illustrate the creative use of microteaching in Jefferson County: The first involves an art teacher who developed an interest in the philosophical implications of the art of teaching. He decided to investigate the effectiveness of three different styles on the art work of his students. The three teaching styles were the authoritarian, the *laissez faire,* and the democratic. To test the effect of these three styles, he set up three microteaching sessions. In each, he used one of the styles to teach a small group of students. All the lessons were taped. At the end he took the art work from all three lessons and put them on faculty bulletin boards. Then he invited his colleagues to judge which works resulted from which teaching styles. The faculty became quite involved in this question. In a special faculty meeting he told them his results and showed them tapes of his three microteaching lessons. Although he learned a great deal from this small experiment, the faculty dialog that ensued was undoubtedly the major payoff.

The second example involved a science teacher. He videotaped a micro-lesson that dealt with the particular methodology for teaching the use of precision balances. The teacher gave the lesson a few times until he had developed a lesson that satisfied him. Instead of erasing the tape, he is now using it in the open laboratory. The tape is one of many resources that students use. Rather than having to teach the use of precision balances over and over again, the teacher simply directs students to review the tape when he thinks they are ready for it.

The Jefferson County schools are an example of how microteaching can be shaped to the needs of the professional personnel in a school district. This particular application of the microteaching process also shows how the creative powers of a faculty will flow if given the necessary support and stimulation.

6-3 MICROTEACHING IN AN INNER-CITY SETTING

Jean Baptiste DuSable High School is one of the oldest high schools in Chicago. It was named after the founder of the city, a Negro. All of the 3600 students who attend DuSable High School are black. The huge three-story school building is bounded by a row of decayed town houses on the Wabash Avenue side and by a large public housing project on the other. The school was built before the days of videotape recorders and air conditioners. On a hot day the temperature hovers between 85 and 90 degrees. Fixed desks, music lessons in the hallway, fire drills, and a crowded summer school all compete with the business at hand: a microteaching clinic.

During the summer of 1968, DuSable High School was the setting for the microteaching phase of the Ford Training and Placement Program, a joint project of the Chicago board of education and the University of Chicago. The aim of the Ford Training and Placement Program is to develop cadres of school personnel—administrators, psychological specialists, social workers, and experienced and beginning teachers—to work together in teams or cadres both to increase their individual competence and to extend their effectiveness through group efforts. The 40 participants in the program spent six weeks of the summer working in three teams, each team in the process of forming a cadre of faculty and staff at a city school the following September. Two cadres were composed of secondary school personnel and one of elementary school personnel. The summer training was designed specifically to prepare the people for their work in inner-city schools. Cadre activities included group problem-solving sessions, curriculum revision, intensive study of each school's surrounding community, and a microteaching clinic. For three weeks, the participants spent three hours a week in microteaching training sessions at the university and five hours a week at the DuSable clinic.

The DuSable microteaching clinic had three main purposes: First, to train teachers in specific teaching skills; second, to provide the cadre members with training in helping one another improve their instructional skills; and third, to provide all the participants with some insight into the teaching process as the teacher perceives it. Since many of the participants, such as the psychological specialists and social workers, had no teaching experience and would have limited opportunities to acquire such experience, microteaching facilitated their getting the feel of the teacher's role. Also, during the summer training program black students and interested community people were hired to act as trainers and resource people for the cadre members. Although all the students took part in the clinic as students, some of the students and some of the community people occasionally tried teaching, with the regular teachers acting as supervisors.

Teaching skills trained included reinforcement, nonverbal cues, and probing, divergent, and higher-order questioning skills. During the third week many teachers opted for a classroom-control sequence in which student teams were "programmed" to misbehave. The object was for the teacher to handle the student behavior problems as smoothly as possible, causing the minimum interruption in the lesson. This practice opportunity was especially valued by the beginning teachers who were concerned about their ability to handle classroom disruptions. It was, of course, the most popular training phase with the students, many of whom revealed a surprising flare for the dramatic. Interestingly, two students chose this option for their own microteaching sessions.

Since a major objective of the total program was to train the cadre members to be able to help one another, the microteaching trainees also served as supervisors. During work in the clinic each cadre member spent approximately half his time as a trainee and half as a supervisor. Training and supervision were aided by a series of tapes made by the clinic director, Dr. Kevin Ryan, and the assistant director, Mrs. Alice Carnes. The tapes depicted a number of encounters between a teacher and a supervisor. Some of the encounters were parodies of poor supervisory techniques and some were examples of effective techniques. In the clinic itself, faculty and staff members from the University of Chicago sat in on the lessons and commented on the supervisory conferences. In effect, they supervised the supervisory conferences.

A third objective of the DuSable clinic—to promote understanding of the teacher's role—was fulfilled through a number of means. The social workers and psychological specialists worked right along with their cadre members. They observed training sessions, planned lessons, taught five-minute lessons, and acted as supervisors. They learned much about the process of teaching, but also brought fresh insights from their own fields to their teacher colleagues. The community people had a rare opportunity to observe and analyze the teaching process. Many made valuable comments to teachers in feedback sessions. A few asked for the opportunity and taught some microteaching sessions.

The response of the cadre members was, in general, enthusiastic. Two teams expressed interest in setting up a clinic at their schools in the fall. They responded positively to the tangible, practical nature of the training. The inexperienced school personnel felt that they had gained much, since the clinic was set in a public school in session, rather than back on the campus. There was some criticism of the five-minute lesson limit, particularly from experienced teachers. Many participants felt that, in order to minimize the repetitive nature of the students' comments, methods of student feedback might have been varied. The suggestion was made that during the first week of the clinic, students might write anonymous reactions, then move to feedback forms during the second week, and finally into oral commentary. Supervision training was perceived as an important facet of the clinic, but one which would have had more effect had there been more staff "supervision of supervision," particularly during the first week.

The videotaping was a near disaster. During the first week there was a frustrating series of equipment breakdowns. Videotape playback was available for only 20% of the lessons. Toward the end the availability improved significantly, but trainees had become used to working without it. Since the microteaching clinic was only one part of a busy and demanding training program, communication among the staff, cadre members, and microteaching students was crucial. To improve communication a mimeographed newspaper entitled the "Mini-Gazette for Maxi-Efficiency" was periodically issued. It included suggestions for improving supervision and teaching skills, announcements and schedule changes, status reports on the health of the videotaping equipment, and a number of other items which helped the clinic move along smoothly.

Conducting a microteaching clinic in an inner-city school was not without difficulties. The difficulties, in their way, matched the benefits. When the videotape recorder was on the blink, when it was 90° in the classrooms, when the firebells rang and the halls filled up with lunchtime crowds, the DuSable clinic kept rolling along. The participants realized that they were not only learning some teaching and supervisory skills, but they were also learning how to cope with life in the urban public school.

6-4 MICROTEACHING IN A SMALL LIBERAL ARTS COLLEGE

The supervisory teacher has a central role in the preparation of teachers. He acts as a model for the beginner. He mediates between the teacher training institution and the student teacher. He helps the student teacher translate his knowledge of the teaching process into classroom practice. Frequently, however, the key role of supervising teacher is carried out poorly, even by excellent teachers. There are several reasons for this: Supervising teachers are chosen for their skill as teachers, and given no training in supervision. They have little understanding of the objectives of the training institution. There is little dialog between the training institution and the supervisor on the progress of the student teacher. When this happens, all suffer, particularly the beginning teacher. He gets caught in a crossfire of divergent intentions and miscommunication.

In 1964 Horace E. Aubertine, then the Director of Teacher Education at Whitman College, Walla Walla, Washington, used microteaching not only to train undergraduates, but also to create a cadre of clinically trained supervising teachers. In establishing the Whitman microteaching clinic, Aubertine set out to investigate two questions in particular:

1. Would the continuity in the teacher training process be improved if the supervising teachers received training in supervision procedures, applied these procedures in microteaching sessions, and then evaluated the outcome?

2. Which areas in the training of clinical supervisors would be most appropriate for the use of microteaching?

Five teachers from the Walla Walla school district were chosen to be supervising teachers and to take part in the microteaching clinic. Their training began a month before Whitman College's full semester period began. During this month of formal training, Aubertine instructed the five teachers in the purposes and functions of the microteaching clinic. He emphasized specific teaching skills, such as set induction, pacing, and continuity. He explained the use of two specially designed feedback-rating forms, and outlined procedures for providing for feedback to beginning teachers in critique sessions.

To facilitate communication and promote the idea of systematic analysis of the variables in teaching and learning, Aubertine also introduced two conceptual models. One, which was developed by Downey,[2] was used for the identification and categorization of the critical variables of the educative process. The second, developed by Aubertine,[3] was used to view the teaching process in a three-stage cyclical analysis. These same conceptual models were taught to the student teachers during the early part of the fall semester.

The Whitman College microteaching clinic was conducted once a week, on Saturdays, at Walla Walla High School. The students for the clinic came from the high school. The school's Future Teachers of America volunteered to work in the clinic without pay. The 20 high school students were broken down into four teams of five each. The clinic was the practicum for Aubertine's methods course. Only student teachers were allowed to enroll and participate as trainees in the clinic. The five supervising teachers who had received training supervised their student teachers for the microteaching sessions.

The Whitman clinic operated for ten consecutive Saturdays each semester. The first three sessions were devoted to diagnosis and training in specific skills of teaching. During the next four sessions each student teacher developed a four-lesson unit, which he taught on consecutive Saturdays. The last three Saturday sessions were remedial sessions for student teachers who needed extra help. The Whitman clinic followed a 15-20-minute-teach, 15-20-minute-critique pattern. There was no re-teach-recritique cycle.

At the end of each Saturday's microteaching, the supervising teachers and Aubertine sat down to examine the progress of the student teachers and the program. During these sessions the supervisors were encouraged to find ways to improve the clinic. Quite a few changes in the clinic resulted from these meetings.

During the first semester Aubertine observed several changes in the supervisor teachers. The ratings of the supervisors became more sensitive to those aspects of the lesson which were likely to have either positive or adverse effects on students. The supervisors assumed the role of listeners and question raisers in the critique sessions. Vague, generalized criticisms dropped off and supervisors began focusing on one or two aspects of a lesson. They encouraged student teachers to share materials more. Lastly, some supervisors invited student teachers to observe *their* classes and hold critique sessions after class.

In reporting on the overall effects of the training of supervising teachers, Aubertine said that "microteaching was worth while in the training of clinical supervisors particularly in development of: a) adroitness in utilizing conceptual models, and in analyzing the teaching process with new insights into the instructional act; b) sophistication in interpreting high school pupils' behavior; c) dexterity in selecting and synthesizing relevant aspects of a lesson; d) expertise in devising and asking probing questions of the student teacher in order to help him analyze his instruction and create alternatives to it; e) facility in human relations, especially in creating rapport with the student-teachers by way of increasing sensitivity to their problems; f) capacity to instill and build confidence within the student teacher."[4]

Both Whitman College and the Walla Walla school district benefited from this microteaching experience. The clinic became a bridge between the college and the schools, acting as the locus for training and communication. Aubertine summarized its effects as follows:

The two-year experience with the Whitman College microteaching clinic indicated that continuity of teacher training was improved and the clinic was considered valuable by supervising teachers and school administrators. The program helped screen out the unfit and made the transition for those qualified to teach less abrupt from college to field phases of training. . . . A high degree of rapport and cooperation was maintained during the two-year period. [5]

6-5 THE TEACHER CORPS

Dr. Jimmie C. Fortune of Memphis State University is currently using microteaching to accomplish several objectives in a Teacher Corps program at his university. The federally supported Teacher Corps program at Memphis State University is a two-year teacher education program for students who hold Bachelor of Science degrees but who have little experience in education as a discipline.

The program, which is designed to train teams of four interns plus a master teacher, is divided into two phases. During the first or pre-service phase, the trainees are enrolled in education and academic courses on campus, and go through a limited internship that provides tutoring and enrichment experiences for culturally disadvantaged children. Microteaching, when used in pre-service training, serves as an introduction to professional education. This introductory course is designed not only to acquaint the intern-trainees with the teaching-learning process, but also to adequately prepare them as tutors for their internship work. During the second or in-service phase, the trainees carry a lighter course load on campus and take on increasing teacher responsibilities as interns in a school. The MSU Teacher Corps program has used microteaching to achieve goals of both the pre-service and in-service programs, and also to function as an important tool with which to evaluate the program.

When the Teacher Corps uses microteaching as part of the introductory course in education, it performs a special screening function. Since Teacher Corps interns are selected with little recourse to the normal screening devices that might indicate future teaching competence, the program directors were concerned about the suitability of the people entering as interns. The Teacher Corps program therefore uses the microteaching experiences as performance criteria during the summer pre-service program. The directors feel that they can gauge a trainee's readiness for in-service work by his performance in microteaching.

In this application of microteaching in the pre-service program, there is a three-hour, two-shift class schedule. The trainees are asked to teach ten-minute lessons, on both assigned and elected subjects, to five elementary students, selected from an enrichment program in the university's campus school and ranging from second to fourth grades. The microteaching sequences include the following: a ten-minute teaching episode; a ten-minute question period in which both the trainee and the master teacher talk informally with the students in order to gain evaluative feedback of the teaching performance; a ten-minute critique and viewing of the videotape by the intern, the master teacher, and a university instructor. After this there is a ten-minute period of reteaching, to a new group of students. Each trainee goes through three of these sequences a week during the five-week summer session. This use of microteaching within the structure of an education course gives the trainees experience with elementary pupils, with content designed for remediation, and with communicating in small groups. The microteaching experiences are directly related to the Teacher Corpsman's work in the field.

The in-service utilization of microteaching
During the in-service phase of training, the intern trainees are busy from Monday to Friday working in schools and return to the campus on Saturdays for special seminars on instructional processes. The Saturday seminars are set up to give the intern trainees a chance to reflect on their experience and to seek solutions to the problems confronting them in schools. Also, since several teams working independently of one another come together on Saturdays, there is the opportunity for cross-germination among teams and for enactment of on-the-job problems and classroom occurrences. Often the interns encounter school situations which tend to be shocking and discouraging. Dr. Fortune, with

wry understatement, describes the situation thus: "These Saturday seminars are not without frustrations. There are moments when disbelief in educational theory seems their only contact with reality."

Microteaching is used in a very informal and flexible way in the Saturday seminars. As problems arise during discussion and staff probing, students are urged to re-enact situations in a microteaching setting. Group discussion replaces the normal supervisory contact. Here colleagues—both master teachers and fellow interns—give the new teacher feedback on performance and suggest alternative strategies.

Utilization of microteaching in program evaluation

The MSU Teacher Corps program is an experimental effort, and therefore efforts are underway to measure the effect of the program on the behavior of the intern trainees. Microteaching is a major part of this evaluative effort. Before he becomes involved in the microteaching course, each trainee is asked to select a topic for a 10-15-minute microteaching lesson which is taught to five students. The trainee is allowed two or three trial performances, each of which is taped; then he selects the performance which he feels is his best. Similar procedures are followed during the summer between the first and second year and at the end of the second year. The evaluation plan involves a random ordering of the tapes after an identification number has been assigned to each. The identification indicates trainee and year of taping. The tapes are then exposed in random order to several educators. These educators rate the tapes, using several appraisal instruments, and make evaluative assessments of the teaching competences shown on each tape. At this writing, the evaluation program has not been completed. According to Fortune, "I will be surprised if large increments of intern behavior-change on most criterion measures are not visible."

6-6 THE PEACE CORPS

Since the normal Peace Corps tour of duty is only two years, teacher training for the Peace Corps must be brief, intensive, and effective. Given the temporal restrictions and the demands for high quality, the directors of the Peace Corps have been especially enthusiastic in adopting microteaching for the training of volunteers. The Peace Corps has found in microteaching not only a means for compressed training in the skills of teaching, but also a way of acculturating volunteers to their role with children of a foreign country. Microteaching was first incorporated into Peace Corps teacher education in the summer of 1966. Two of those microteaching clinics will be described here.

Peace Corps training for the Philippines

Stanford University was the site of a Peace Corps training program for 49 volunteers preparing for assignments in the Philippines. The volunteers were to be readied to assist Filipino teachers in elementary schools. In particular, the volunteers were to be trained to teach English as a second language to children whose native tongue is Tagalog. A major portion of the training program was devoted to microteaching. The objectives of the clinic were: (1) to equip the volunteers with teaching skills directly related to teaching English as a second language; and (2) to acquaint them with special materials for teaching English as a second language. However, there was an overall objective of training to which the microteaching contributed substantially: Stated simply, it was to give the trainees a "reality test." David Evans, the director of the Peace Corps Microteaching Clinic, stated it this way:

The trainees are faced from the very start with the need to deal with children, and ideally Filipino children who are speaking Tagalog constantly. Each trainee must almost daily deal with the questions, "Do I want to be a teacher? Do I like children? Can I communicate with them, and do I want to become an elementary school teacher for two years?" These are difficult questions, particularly for the boys coming from the American collegiate atmosphere where children are non-existent, where teaching has low status, where elementary teaching has negative status in that it is perceived as an exclusively female occupation. Eating with small children, having to hold their trays, stopping them from fighting, realizing how easily they can get hurt, and the responsibility that goes with watching children, seeing how much continued attention they take, trying to talk to them or keep them entertained—all these things are new for the trainee. Virtually none of them can be transmitted verbally and for that reason are not dealt with in the more traditional training programs.

To achieve their objectives and to make the microteaching clinic as realistic as possible, the directors decided to find Filipino children for the clinic. After several months of combing the San Francisco Bay area, they discovered several pockets of newly arrived Filipino families. When the parents were told how their children could help prepare teachers for the Philippines, and that the children would receive special training in English, they readily agreed to let their children act as students. Each day, for the five weeks of the clinic, 20 children ranging in age from five to twelve were picked up by bus and brought to the campus. As soon as they arrived the children were given lunch, and then became students in the clinic. For the half-day in the clinic the children were paid $1.50. Although their attitude may possibly be attributed to their getting paid, nevertheless the newly arrived Filipino children seemed to enjoy their young teachers and this new type of schooling. Absenteeism was almost nonexistent.

Another boon to the Stanford Peace Corps training program was the use of volunteers fresh back from the Philippines as supervisors in the clinic. Since they had just completed their tour of duty, their Philippines experience was vivid in their minds. Their presence, too, lent an air of reality to the total program. These returnees could speak with authority about the role of a Peace Corpsman in the Philippines. Having worked as teacher assistants in the elementary schools, they were familiar with the materials for teaching English as a second language and the problems related to the task. They were able to describe how the Philippines schools are run and how to work with the native teachers. Although the returnees took on this new task of supervisor with a great depth of knowledge about the Philippines and high prestige among the new volunteers, they had little or no experience as supervisors of teachers. Also, the microteaching clinic and the operating principles underlying it were totally foreign to them.

In the weeks prior to the arrival of the volunteers, the returnee-supervisors underwent special training for their work in the microteaching clinic, including actually teaching in the clinic. Besides teaching and being supervised, they took turns supervising one another. Here, too, their performance was critically analyzed. During the initial weeks of training it became clear that the returnees as a group had special problems as supervisors. Much of their training dealt with the following five issues:

First, the new supervisors tended to be exclusively negative in their criticism. Their natural styles had to be changed so that they were more supporting, warm and critical in a positive way. Second, they tended to think that comments such as "Don't drill beyond point of interest" would be enough to change a trainee's behavior. The returnees had to assume a more analytical approach to teaching and one that dealt with the specific behaviors of teaching. Third, the skills that were to be taught in the clinic needed very definite clarification for the supervisors. Although they had been teaching English as a second language, the component skills still needed pointing out and highlighting. Fourth, they tended to criticize too much, sometimes finding six or seven weaknesses in a five-minute teaching session. The principle of focusing on one or two points was easily understood but difficult to put into practice. Like many experienced supervisors, these returnees had an almost uncontrollable urge to demonstrate the breadth of their knowledge and "tell all." Fifth, the trainees were unfamiliar with the videotape system and tended to misuse it. They had to be trained to use it as a teaching tool, going over specific parts of the tape that advanced the goals of their supervision.

Throughout the duration of the microteaching clinic, the supervisors met to continue training. These meetings dealt with the techniques of supervision, the principles of behavior change, and the problems that were facing them in the day-to-day operation of the clinic. Also, the supervisors worked together to develop the rating-feedback forms, plus model tapes of specific skills in the teaching of English as a second language.

Stanford Peace Corps directors took the starch out of the normal microteaching structure. Although they freely borrowed from past procedures, they nevertheless made extensive innovations in format. They first decided what they wanted the microteaching clinic to accomplish, and then designed a structure that complemented these goals. The microteaching clinic operated for seven of the nine weeks that comprised the first stage of the volunteers' training program. Four different formats were used. The first format was the traditional five-minute lesson, followed by a ten-minute critique, which in turn was followed by a reteach and a recritique. This phase lasted for three weeks, and each volunteer had nine half-hour experiences. The lessons focused on a variety of simple skills and techniques related to teaching English as a second language. Immediately after this three-week period, the entire training program moved to Stockton, California, a community with a substantial Filipino population, for two weeks. The volunteers spent the first week in the classes of minority-group children in Stockton elementary schools. Here they observed the classes, helped the teachers, and not infrequently took over the entire class for short periods of teaching. The second week in Stockton the trainees worked in community projects of their own design.

When they returned to the campus, they entered the second phase of microteaching, which had a different format: This time the volunteers taught 20-minute lessons followed by a 10-minute critique. There was no reteach or recritique. Each volunteer taught four sequential lessons to the same children. Also, during this week, volunteers were encouraged to observe one another's teaching.

During the third phase of the clinic, which was the fifth week of microteaching, the format reverted to the teach-reteach pattern, with only one variation. This time the lessons were between 8 and 10 minutes in length and the critique periods were shortened to 5 and 7 minutes. During this week the focus was on the skills of teaching reading. The reading lessons were lengthened to 8 to 10 minutes to enable the volunteers to have the pupils read short paragraphs or do other activities.

The final two-week phase had a radically different format. Three people—two volunteers and one supervisor-returnee—were grouped together for coteaching. The groups were composed of people who had had relatively little contact with one another. The purpose was to simulate a situation faced by the newly arrived volunteer in the field. The supervisor was instructed to play the role of a Philippine teacher and build into the final weeks some of the difficulties the volunteers would soon be facing. Although all three were involved in planning lessons, the two volunteers took on the major teaching tasks. The groups worked in one-hour blocks, devoting the first 30 minutes to teaching sequential lessons and the second 30 minutes to a critique and planning session. During this phase the volunteers taught classes of 12 children, who stayed with them for the entire sequence.

The flexible format used by the Peace Corps clinic seemed to work quite smoothly. Volunteers had the chance to teach under a variety of conditions. As Evans stated in his final report:

In summary, one can see the progression of complexities which the trainees were called upon to cope with in teaching. Beginning with a highly simplified situation of five minutes and four pupils and only a very simple objective, they moved to larger classes, longer lessons, more demanding subject matter, and finally to a complex interpersonal situation in which to make teaching decisions.

The Peace Corps clinic at Stanford, the first large-scale use of microteaching in the preparation of volunteers, has become a model for other Peace Corps training programs. It's also an example of tailoring a training protocol to training objectives, and not vice versa.

Peace Corps microteaching for Micronesia

Perhaps it was inevitable that the Peace Corps training program for Micronesia could not resist microteaching. Certainly it has been difficult to exclude the Micronesia experience from this volume. The decision to include microteaching in the Peace Corps Micronesia training program was made rather late in the summer of 1966. The Micronesia program, like the Stanford-Philippines, was designed to prepare volunteers for the role of teaching English as a second language. However, microteaching did not have a central place in its program, as it did in the one on the Stanford campus. A month before the program got underway in Key West, Florida, James Cooper was invited to set up and direct a three-week clinic for 330 volunteers. There was very little opportunity to carefully plan the program. The small staff of ten people was totally unfamiliar with microteaching, and the physical conditions were far from ideal. However, Cooper demonstrated that microteaching can exist and excel even under the most adverse conditions.

The microteaching clinic was set up in the bath house of the Casa Marina Hotel on the outskirts of Key West. One week before the arrival of the volunteers the bath house was converted into 12 small classrooms, each large enough to hold three volunteers, a supervisor, four children and a blackboard. Unfortunately, the construction and renovation of the bath house continued during the operation of the clinic, which hardly added to the clinic's effectiveness. Also, the late summer heat of southern Florida kept the classrooms hot and muggy.

The 330 volunteers came with little or no teaching experience. Their aim was to learn the skills and materials of teaching English as a second language. They were divided into seven groups, representing the seven different island groups within Micronesia. Each group had special language training. During the three weeks of microteaching, each group was away on field work for one week. Therefore each volunteer could receive only six microteaching experiences, three times in one week and three in the other.

The students for the microteaching clinic were recruited from local families. Many of these children were Cuban refugees and spoke little or no English. Others were native Key West children, but of Spanish-speaking backgrounds. The children worked in two shifts, a morning shift from 8 to 11 A.M. and an afternoon shift from 1 to 4 P.M. Altogether, there were approximately 70 children between the ages of 5 and 15. They were arranged into groups of three, according to age and ability to speak English. Thus for both the morning and afternoon there were 12 teams of students, one group for each classroom. While some knew the rudiments of reading and writing English, others had no English skills at all. One of the objectives of the program was to provide some real language training for these children. In addition, the children were paid 50¢ a day for their three hours in the clinic.

Since there was only one videotape recorder—a small home recorder—the decision was made to use it for instructing the volunteers, instead of as a means for feedback in the clinic. This decision freed the staff, enabling them to devote more time to supervising in the clinic. During odd hours the staff taped lessons for later presentation to the volunteers. These lessons varied from theoretical considerations of language teaching to tips on teaching technique. Many dealt directly with the volunteers' task in microteaching.

The clinic format was structured so that two volunteers shared an hour. One would start teaching a brief 5- or 10-minute lesson. At the end of the lesson the supervisor and the two volunteers would critique it. Then the second volunteer would teach a brief lesson, followed by a critique. Since the children were not changed, the reteach lessons were extensions of the first lessons. This format allowed each volunteer to teach two lessons and observe two lessons within an hour. It also built into the clinic continuity of learning for the children. Since an important consideration was the instruction given to the children, an effort was made to make each hour instructionally integral. Also, each hour was one in a sequence. This format was used for the length of the clinic.

While Cooper and his staff found many barriers to developing the full potential of microteaching and recommended several changes for future use, the clinic was apparently a great success with the volunteers. Cooper states:

Despite the difficulties involved, the Volunteers virtually unanimously declared microteaching to have been an extremely valuable part of their training. Ninety-seven per cent of the Volunteers felt microteaching was valuable or extremely valuable in their preparation for teaching. Over ninety-five per cent of the Volunteers recommended microteaching experience for future trainees. The very few who were not satisfied with microteaching were those who did not have a regular teacher of English as a second language as a supervisor.

6-7 MICROTEACHING IN A PROGRAM TO IMPROVE COLLEGE TEACHING

Higher education does not have a strong tradition of giving formal attention to the process of teaching. Most college instructors are graduated from institutions which give little or no training in how to teach. Compared with elementary and secondary school teachers, college teachers have a heightened sense that teaching is a private, personal concern. However, the growing discontent over the quality of college teaching among students, administrators, and college teachers themselves may be a harbinger of change on the campus.

During the 1966-67 academic year, two professors at the University of Illinois, Arye Perlberg and D. C. O'Bryant, conducted a study to explore ways to improve college teaching.* Microteaching and the analysis of videotapes of classrooms were the primary means for improving instruction. However, both were integrated into larger training sequences. The study conducted by Perlberg and O'Bryant was carried on in the Department of General Engineering at the Urbana campus. Sensitive to college teachers' suspicion of training in teaching, Perlberg and O'Bryant worked to develop activities for which faculty members would volunteer. Microteaching was used in two different training sequences. In both cases microteaching was only a part of a larger effort to improve instruction.

The first training sequence was called the "Individual Model." It was designed to explore patterns of helping relationships between senior faculty members and an educational consultant. A senior faculty member in the department—a full professor—volunteered to receive help to improve his teaching. For this small pilot study, the professor chose a course in the history of technology, a subject which he saw as lending itself to critical analysis of technological developments and synthesis with his students' humanistic education. The professor believed strongly that interaction with the students was very important, and to reach these ends, he had always divided his normal class of 40 into two groups of 20. His sole purpose for increasing his own work load was to facilitate classroom discussion. Early in the study an analysis of tape recordings of the professor's class revealed that his style of teaching was lecture-centered. Occasionally he asked a "Who?" or "When?" question. Almost all the lecture material and the answers to his questions were to be found in the course textbook. After analysis of the first tape recordings of his "classroom discussion," he and the consultant decided to concentrate on improving his questioning techniques. He told his students that they were expected to read the textbook

---

* Perlberg, Arye, and D. C. O'Bryant, *Video Recording and Microteaching Techniques to Improve Engineering Instruction,* Urbana, Ill.: University of Illinois, 1968, mimeographed.

material before class. He also assigned them specific analytical questions which were to be the basis for classroom discussion. He then rearranged his classroom. He unbolted the chairs and desks and changed them from their rows and columns to a horseshoe-shaped arrangement. Each week one of his three sessions was taped and analyzed with the consultant. Further, he volunteered for some micro-lessons in the College of Education's microteaching laboratory. During these microteaching sessions special attention was given to higher-order questioning, the encouragement of student questioning, and the skills of involving timid students and calming down those who made a habit of monopolizing the discussion. He also worked to improve his nonverbal communication skills.

The professor was quite satisfied with these activities. His classes changed markedly, which was obvious to both the professor and the students. He practiced his newly discovered teaching skills at home, with the help of his wife. Evaluation of his tapes by the research team, live observation in his classroom, and discussion by the researchers with his students indicated a definite change in teaching style.

The second sequence of microteaching was part of the training of teaching assistants in engineering graphics. For some years new staff members teaching this course had attended a weekly in-service course, which dealt primarily with subject matter. With the addition of microteaching and videotape, the course was extended to two meetings weekly, with one session devoted entirely to the process of teaching. Four new teaching assistants took part in the training. During their weekly meetings, their own classes in engineering graphics were taped and analyzed with the help of a consultant. Each assistant identified a teaching problem and worked with the consultants to overcome it.

The group used microteaching as a trial run for subject matter to be taught the following week. Each assistant taught a 20-minute lesson to five students. The consultants, Perlberg and O'Bryant, acted as supervisors. After each lesson the paid learners, the other teaching assistants and the consultants provided the teaching assistant with feedback, using an evaluative instrument. Also, the teaching assistants and the consultants reviewed the taped lesson and the feedback during their in-service training time. Each micro-lesson, then, was gone over twice.

Although the University of Illinois' use of microteaching was more in the nature of a pilot study than a full-blown application, the pioneering quality of the work makes it worthy of reporting. In all, 16 faculty members took part. Most indicated readiness to pursue such work the next year. More important, however, this application of microteaching demonstrates the careful, graduated approach necessary when moving into a new area, such as the training of college teachers.

6-8 A MICROTEACHING CLINIC FOR COLLEGE TEACHERS

Although the resistance to some type of teacher education for those preparing for careers in higher education is beginning to crack, few college teachers have yet to benefit directly. However, there is a growing concern on the nation's campuses for quality teaching. Methods are being sought to provide highly relevant, effective, and concentrated training for potential college teachers. Microteaching is one such method.

In the spring of 1967, at the request of the American Society for Engineering Education, Dr. Merritt A. Williamson, professor of Engineering Management at Vanderbilt University, conducted a three-day workshop in Nashville for college teachers. The 20 participants came from the following predominantly Negro institutions: Tennessee A & I State University, A & I College, Greensboro, N. C.; Tuskegee Institute; Southern University; and Prairie View A & M College. Mr. David B. Young and Mr. James M. Cooper of Stanford University's microteaching staff were invited to conduct the microteaching clinic, which was held concurrently with the lectures and workshops presented by a staff of outstanding educators who came from four different institutions.

A few weeks before the workshop, each participant was sent a description of microteaching and was asked to prepare a 10-minute lesson for the workshop. The students used in the workshop microteaching clinic were undergraduates majoring in engineering. The students, all of whom volunteered their services, were divided into groups of nine each. Since all the students were from the same institution (Tennessee A & I State University), as were many of the workshop participants, the directors were concerned that this could be an inhibiting factor. The college professors to whom the students were familiar felt just the opposite. They felt that the opportunity to practice teaching with students they knew gave them an advantage which the other participants did not have.

The three-day workshop was devoted to lecture-discussions and microteaching. Since Young and Cooper were directing the microteaching part of the conference themselves, they could not provide microteaching experiences for all the participants at the same time. Therefore a format was developed in which the microteaching clinic ran concurrently with the lecture-discussions for two of the three days. This meant that each participant missed a portion of the lecture-discussion program while he was involved in microteaching.

The skill chosen for the workshop was varying the stimulus situation, as discussed in Chapter 2. This skill, which in many ways is simply the knitting together of several discrete skills, was chosen not only because of its relationship to good teaching, but also because it dramatizes the power of microteaching. Teachers can usually make very dramatic gains in the performance of this skill. They can see very vividly how they have changed in their behavior. This, indeed, was the case at this workshop for college teachers.

The clinic was structured as follows: Each participant taught a 10-minute diagnostic lesson which he had previously prepared. The lessons were taped, the students and supervisors filled out feedback forms, and a 10-minute critique followed, consisting of both oral and written instructions in varying the stimulus situation. At this point, once the behaviors to be demonstrated were clarified, the college teacher had a half-hour break before beginning the reteach-recritique cycle. Then he taught the same lesson again to a different group of nine students. During the break he reviewed the information received in the critique session and reread the instructional material on varying the stimulus situation. After the second 10-minute period of teaching, feedback data were collected and studied and the new videotapes were reviewed.

Professor Williamson followed up the workshop by a thorough evaluative survey. The survey revealed that microteaching was judged by the participants to be a unanimous success. Although 12 of the 19 who filled out the appraisal form indicated that they were apprehensive about participating in the microteaching clinic, all the participants agreed that it was a very helpful experience. Also, all 19 concurred in the statement that they would recommend microteaching experiences for other teachers, and that they would like to do more microteaching at later workshops. Many of the college teachers wrote additional comments about the experience. One reported, "The workshop to me was like looking into a mirror at myself as a *teacher* of engineering. The reflection served as self-evaluation, and will help me to be a more effective teacher."

6-9 MICRO-COUNSELING

Teaching beginning counselors "how to counsel" normally suffers the same fate as teacher education: a great deal of talk, but little action. Like teaching, counseling has too long been viewed as an almost mystical art which the counselor has acquired through prayer and fasting. As a result, counselor training generally has been neither very effective nor economical of human resources. A large portion of counselor training consists of being told "how to counsel." Much of this talk has been diffuse, time-consuming, and vague.

Recently Allen Ivey and four colleagues at Colorado State College at Fort Collins applied the microteaching framework to the training of counselors. In what Ivey and his colleagues call "micro-counseling," counselor trainees systematically practice component skills of counseling. The counselor trainee practices single skills in brief counseling sessions. The trainee, instead of working with a small class, works with a single client. Feedback is collected from the supervisor, the trainee, and the client. Sessions are also videotaped. Ivey and his colleagues used microteaching "to provide pre-practicum training and, thus, bridge the gap between classroom theory and actual practice."[*]

Three controlled research studies involving micro-counseling were conducted at the Fort Collins campus. The intention of the studies was to test the effectiveness of micro-counseling in training for three skills:

---

[*] Allen Ivey, Cheryl J. Normington, C. Dean Miller, Weston H. Morrill, and Richard F. Haase, "Micro-Counseling and Attending Behavior," in *Journal of Counseling Psychology,* 1968.

attending behavior, Rogerian reflection of feeling, and summarization of feeling. The first study dealt with attending behavior of counselors, which is considered to be one of the basic dimensions of the counseling process. Attending behavior is the counseling skill of attending to or listening to a client both verbally and nonverbally. One of the basic tasks of counselor training is to help the neophyte counselor relax, pay attention to the client, and refrain from jumping from topic to topic. Therefore it seemed appropriate that the counselor skill first focused on would be attending behavior, which helps the counselor be attentive and communicate his attentiveness to his client. To master the skill of attending behavior, the trainees were told to practice three component behaviors while working with their clients. The three are: *first,* eye contact, in which the counselor simply looks at the client; *second,* gestures, movements, and posture positions which communicate attentiveness; and *third,* verbal attention, which is indicated by the counselor responding to the last comment of the client without introducing new data of his own.

The second in the series of three studies involved the skill of reflecting feelings. Empathetic understanding and communication of warmth and genuineness are essential to the successful counselor. Particularly important to these qualities is what Carl Rogers calls the skill of reflection of feelings. This skill was chosen because it plays an important part in communicating to the client that "I am with you—I can accurately sense the world as you are feeling and perceiving it." In many counseling programs this skill is considered to be essential to the effective counselor. However, teaching the skill often proves to be one of the counselor-educator's most difficult tasks.

Micro-counseling treats reflection of feeling as a type of attending behavior in which the counselor *selectively attends* to one certain aspect (or aspects) of his interaction with the client. For instance, he may focus on a particular emotional state. Viewed from this perspective, much of the complexity in the reflection of feeling disappears, and it becomes possible to teach the skill to a counselor trainee in the standard microteaching framework.

The third skill, summarization of feelings, can be considered as an extension of attending behavior and the reflection of feelings. However, in this case, the counselor is attending to a broader class of stimuli and must have the skill to bring seemingly diverse elements into a meaningful whole. This is achieved when the counselor summarizes the client's comments, relating them to a central theme.

In each of these three studies the group of counselor trainees using microteaching significantly improved their ability to perform the skills. In addition, the investigators report that the trainees found the experience a vital and a far-reaching one. "I spend too much time thinking about what I should say instead of simply listening to the other person." Another stated, "I could have been giving much more to the students I work with—I have been worrying about myself too much."

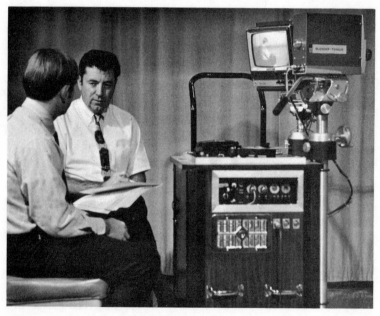

Recorded microteaching lessons may be used for training supervisors, developing and testing new rating protocols, and other analyses. The critique session may immediately follow the lesson, or may not. Results of the critique have been satisfactory with up to four weeks' delay between the teaching and critique sessions. Such delays are particularly relevant when supervisors are not present during the actual teaching session, or when the trainee uses self-critique initially, and later checks his judgment against the supervisor's.

Several mentioned that the skills, particularly attending behavior, proved quite useful in their regular interpersonal relationships.

Ivey feels that many skills of counseling—such as test explanation, information-giving, interpretation, and others—can also be precisely defined and taught within a micro-counseling context. An important implication of these studies is that the skills were learned within a very brief time. Each of the skills was acquired within a two-hour period.

Allen Ivey summarizes the implications and future of his research at the University of Massachusetts as follows:

Most counselor-educators have spent long hours training beginners in the skills of counseling, and most would agree that training neophyte counselors in these skills is a difficult and taxing task. Micro-counseling training seems to provide a framework to make professional counselor training and the training of lay counselors more meaningful and effective. Further, this type of training may be equally important to the teacher, the administrator and the student. The microteaching and micro-counseling framework may be the means by which the developmental skills of living may be taught.

REFERENCES

1. Kallenbach, Warren, "The Effectiveness of Microteaching in the Preparation of Elementary Intern Teachers." Paper delivered at 1968 AERA Convention, February 1968

2. Downey, Lawrence W., *The Secondary Phase of Education.* New York: Blaisdell, 1965, 233 pages.

3. Aubertine, Horace E., *An Experiment in the Set Induction Process and Its Application in Teaching.* Unpublished doctoral dissertation, School of Education, Stanford University, 1964, 140 pages.

4. Aubertine, Horace E., "The Use of Microteaching in Training Supervising Teachers," *High School Journal,* **51**,.2, November 1967.

5. *Ibid.*

Chapter 7
Research and Microteaching

7-1 INTRODUCTION

One of the chief obstacles to definitive research on the teaching act is the immense complexity of the typical classroom situation. The large number of students in a typical classroom, the length of time devoted to a typical classroom session, and the complex nature of the variables inherent in any school situation make the classroom an unfavorable climate for precise research. Thus one of the major attractions of the microteaching format is that it simplifies the teaching act and provides opportunities for real experimental control and manipulation of variables. As a technique for research, microteaching suggests almost limitless combinations of variables for experimentation. This chapter cannot possibly cover all the possible uses of microteaching as a tool for research. However, we shall suggest some divergent issues that can be investigated by means of microteaching in the hopes that other educators will begin to see the enormous research potential inherent in microteaching as a training technique.

There are three broad categories which, at this point in time, represent the areas in which microteaching is most likely to be used to conduct research: *First,* the search for optimal teacher training procedures for use within a microteaching setting; *second,* more general research on training procedures and human learning; and *third,* systematic analysis of the relationship between teacher behaviors and student behaviors. The remainder of this chapter will deal in some detail with each of these three areas of research and, when appropriate, will suggest exemplary research projects and designs. Undoubtedly, as microteaching becomes more widespread as a research and training process, it will suggest other categories of research.

7-2 OPTIMIZING THE TRAINING VALUE OF MICROTEACHING

As a teacher training technique, microteaching is in its early stages. There are many issues related to the most effective use of microteaching for helping new teachers which have yet to be resolved by careful research. A typical microteaching training sequence designed to improve a teacher's competence in the use of a particular skill might be diagrammed this way.

Figure one

T-1	C-1	T R	T-2	C-2

The teacher teaches a brief lesson to a small number of students and tries to highlight a relevant teaching skill (T-1). The teacher, with some kind of supervision, views the videotape of his performance, and then receives feedback on how successfully he performed the teaching skill (C-1). The teacher has a block of time to plan his next lesson, incorporate the feedback from his previous teaching lesson, or receive training (T R). He then teaches the lesson over again to a different group of students in an attempt to improve on his previous use of the skill (T-2). Again he receives feedback by watching the videotape of his second teaching performance, again with some kind of supervision (C-2). The sequence of teaching, critique, and training can be repeated as many times as necessary to bring the teacher up to a pre-set standard of performance of the skill being trained.

Within the framework of such a training format, there are important questions, which could be investigated through systematically designed research activities, about the nature and sequence of the elements. For example, there is no convincing research evidence regarding the optimal length of the microteaching sessions, nor the optimal number of students to be used in them. It may, in fact, be the case that different numbers of students and different time periods are appropriate for training different teaching skills. These issues could be easily investigated by providing identical microteaching training to several groups of teacher trainees while systematically varying the length of the microteaching session and the number of students in those sessions across the various groups.

Similarly, the characteristics of the students used in each teaching session can have a powerful impact on the success or failure of the training. The age, sex, and academic backgrounds of the microteaching students can be varied systematically to determine the optimal mixture for training each of the various teaching skills. Even more interesting is the question of the extent to which the micro-class students should be informed of the nature of the training which their teachers are receiving. What effect does it have on the training of a teacher in a given skill for his micro-class students to know precisely what skill he is trying to learn? Can the training value of microteaching be increased appreciably by informing the micro-class students regarding those teaching skills, and encouraging them to actively help in training the teacher to use them (e.g., by reacting favorably when the teacher does, in fact, use the skill in his microteaching session)? Systematic inspection of such questions could add greatly to our knowledge of the most efficient ways to use the microteaching situation for training purposes.

A second set of considerations about the effective use of microteaching as a training procedure centers around the critique. The key issue here is to make most effective use of the self-confrontation and the feedback it supplies in training teachers to acquire specific teaching skills. For example, would such feedback situations be more effective in changing the teacher's performance if the teacher were required to view his previous performance more than once? (This has been done.) Is the feedback more effective if the videotape is played straight through, or if the teacher trainee can stop it at any point and focus on particular sequences of his behavior? Partial answers to these questions have been obtained in research on self-confrontation in a military training context. The critique session, of course, also provides an opportunity for more fundamental research on the nature of the supervisory process itself. These issues, however, because of their more general nature will be taken up in the following section, which considers microteaching as a means for more general research on human learning.

Finally, there is a whole series of issues that should be investigated related to the timing and sequencing of events. The length of the training session, for example, could have a strong impact on the amount of change produced in the teacher's performance by the entire microteaching session. Furthermore, the sequencing of teaching, critique, and training sessions should be investigated. Some skills, or some training methods (e.g., modeling), may have a more powerful impact on the teacher if the training session immediately follows the teaching session rather than the critique session, as diagrammed in Figure 2.

Figure two

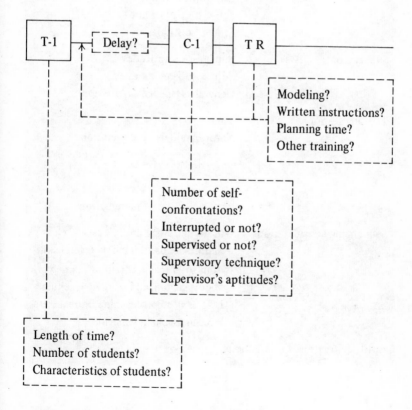

Table one

Teaching skill criteria	General
	Content specific
	Teaching style prerequisites

Trainee's aptitudes

Teaching sessions:	Time
	Number of students
	Students' characteristics
	Students' roles

Critique sessions:	Number of self-viewings
	Interrupted or not
	Self-critiqued or not
	Student critiques

Supervision:	Supervisor's aptitudes
	Supervisor's techniques
	General vs. special supervision

Training sessions:	Time
	Nature, models Exaggeration
	Positive vs. negative
	examples
	Written instructions
	Planning time

Sequencing consideration: Within microteaching
                                Simultaneous training of several skills
                             Within total teacher training framework
                                Microteaching and student teaching
                                Effects of microteaching on real class-
                                   room teaching behavior

Aptitude-treatment interactions

Two crucial points should be made about the kind of research questions mentioned in this section. First, although all these proposed investigations concern the effectiveness of microteaching as a teacher training technique, none of them asks, "Is microteaching a better teacher training technique than something else?" That question is not asked because it is not answerable in that form. The effectiveness of microteaching as a training technique can be evaluated only in relation to a particular teaching skill, and with attention paid to the kind of variables mentioned in Table 1.

Thus, instead of the general question of how effective microteaching is, we need to ask more relevant questions, such as: In teaching a particular skill to a trainee with given aptitudes, what arrangements of teaching sessions, critique sessions, and training sessions are optimal in bringing him to meet a pre-set criterion of performance? There are bodies of research literature that will supply useful hints in both framing and answering such questions (e.g., task analysis research, mass versus space practice research, basic learning research, and research on the sociology of groups). But the important point is that evaluation of microteaching as a teacher training technique must proceed via a careful investigation of the contribution of each of its components. Each component of microteaching must be judged according to how it contributes to the designing of specific training sequences for teachers with different aptitude profiles.

Second, the microteaching situation as described in this section is an excellent microcosmic example of a self-modifying training procedure. That is, microteaching supplies a framework in which research evidence can quite readily feed back into training practice, and in which training practice can open up doors for research. We can expect that, although microteaching will continue to be used for training purposes, it will also form the setting for research which can so modify future teacher training practices that they will provide much better conditions for individual teacher trainees to learn in.

7-3 GENERAL TRAINING AND HUMAN LEARNING RESEARCH
The abovementioned kinds of self-modifying research represent one of the primary strengths of the microteaching situation as a research vehi-

cle. In addition, however, microteaching is a promising road toward studying the process of human learning in general. Both the critique and the training sessions in a typical microteaching block provide chances, in a very controlled situation, to investigate the parameters which affect human learning. The possibilities for such research are limitless, and we wish here to suggest only a few examples.

Some of the most interesting aspects of learning which microteaching can throw light on involve the use of models in the training of specific teaching skills. The social learning work of Bandura[1] is relevant here. Some of the key issues that ought to be investigated include: (1) Is a model of a skill a more efficient aid to learning if it contains both positive and negative instances of the skill, or only the positive? (2) To what extent does extreme exaggeration of teaching techniques in a model add to or detract from its usefulness in a training situation? (3) Is a teacher trainee's ability to transfer the skill to the real classroom improved by the use of models in several different contextual situations (e.g., one in a microteaching situation, one in a regular classroom, and one in a large group lecture hall)? (4) Are modeling procedures more effective in producing learning if they contain segments that show the model being reinforced for performing the desired skill?

Our preliminary research with microteaching indicates that modeling can be a very powerful instrument in the training session. Hence these questions about the specific nature of modeling are of high priority. In addition, the fact that there is a training block in the microteaching sequence gives one a chance to study different training procedures in a controlled situation. Programmed instruction manuals, computer-assisted instruction sequences, lectures, seminars, and many other techniques can be inserted in the training sessions as a way of evaluating their effectiveness in the training of specific teaching skills.

The supervisory sessions enable us to investigate some basic learning phenomena related to self-confrontation situations. We can examine supervisory techniques in a controlled way, to determine the generalizability of basic learning research to a complex human situation. The following list offers a few ideas as to kinds of issues that one can investigate through the supervisory sessions in a microteaching situation: (1) The effectiveness of various schedules of reinforcement in training particular skills. (2) The effectiveness of different verbal and nonverbal reinforcers in training particular skills. (3) The relative training effectiveness of pointing out positive and/or negative instances of a training use of a particular skill in a self-confrontation situation. (4) The effects of training of different attitudinal sets and expectancy on the part of a supervisor. (5) Supervisory techniques and cuing devices which can eventually eliminate the role of the supervisor and make the trainee himself an adequate critic of his own teaching behavior.

The above ideas, may we remind our reader, are only exemplary. The point is that the supervisory session in a microteaching training situation opens up new possibilities for controlled investigation of many basic aspects of human learning.

The whole structure of the microteaching process can be manipulated in order to answer some fundamental questions about sequencing and timing of the practice, modeling, and feedback stages in the learning process. To determine the effects of the delay of feedback on human learning, rest periods of varying lengths can be inserted between the teach and critique sessions. The sequence of practice, modeling, and feedback sessions can be permuted so that empirical data may be gathered; from these data, one can build and evaluate models of the human learning process which incorporate those three elements. Furthermore, through manipulation of the content and sequence of microteaching experiences, the process of self-confrontation, self-analysis, and self-editing of behavior can be analyzed in a controlled and systematic manner.

The point here is that the microteaching situation not only constitutes a powerful training device with the capability of efficient self-modification, but it opens the door for experimentation on the process of learning itself. The kind of experimental control, manipulation, and simplification which microteaching lends itself to can go a long way toward providing an atmosphere in which complex aspects of human life can be examined.

7-4 THE TEACHER-STUDENT INTERACTION
Perhaps the most obvious problem facing any teacher education program is finding some way to relate teacher performance to student

performance. Ideally the skills, attitudes, and understanding which a teacher training program requires of its trainees would be supported by strong empirical evidence of their efficacy in producing learning. Now, however, there is no such empirical base. The objectives of teacher training programs, though they make good intuitive sense, have not been empirically related to their effects on students in the real classroom. And although such intuitions can be a helpful guide for research, they cannot stand alone as guides to practice. Behavioral engineers, however, are conducting research that is forming such a data base, and teacher trainers must soon come to grips with the problem of determining the relationships between teacher performance and student performance so that they can build empirically based justification for the objectives of their training programs. The microteaching situation offers one promising avenue.

For example, one can construct microteaching situations in which both the teacher and students are recorded simultaneously on videotape. It then becomes possible to analyze the effects of various kinds of teacher behavior on the learning and behavior of the micro-class students. Consider the following case in point: One of the skills often trained through the microteaching process is "varying the stimulus situation." This skill includes a variety of teacher behaviors aimed at relieving boredom in the classroom, such as switching back and forth between visual and oral presentation, moving around the classroom, using extravagant arm and body gestures, and changing voice inflection. There is an intuitive basis for believing that a teacher who employs such techniques in the classroom is more likely to attract the attention of his students; there is even some empirical evidence at a more basic level (e.g., the works of Berlyne[2] and Sokolov[3]) which suggest that this skill is effective in producing learning. But the leap from studying rats and the orienting response to studying the effectiveness of varying the stimulus as a teaching skill is an uncomfortable one. The point is, however, that a microteaching situation with simultaneous recording of teacher and student behaviors could be used to study that relationship. With such videotapes, raters could note instances of the skill and at the same time look for various student responses in order to tie the teaching skill to its immediate effect on student behavior, and then measure the achievement of the micro-class students to determine the more long-range effects of the teaching skill on student learning.

One can't overestimate the importance of this kind of research for long-term improvement of teaching. One of the recurring themes in education these days is the insistence on basing the educational process on performance rather than time criteria. Many innovative teacher education programs are therefore in the process of developing performance criteria for teachers, so that certification, training, and promotion can be based on teachers' ability to meet certain pre-set criteria rather than their length of service in the classroom or their accumulated course credits. This movement toward performance rather than length of time in instruction may be one of the most important trends in twentieth century education. But unless research becomes the basis for adopting and rejecting teacher performance criteria, we may find that the whole movement has been from one set of bad intuitions to another. If, on the other hand, our intuitions about teaching performance can be followed up by good research programs, with microteaching as one possible setting for them, then we may turn out teachers with skills and abilities which really do make them better able to guide their students through the learning process. Thus teacher training institutions must certainly begin with a careful task analysis of the components of the teaching act, but there can be no justifiable confidence in their procedures until they have empirically demonstrated the effects of the components of teacher training on the learning of students.

The development of criteria for teaching skill through the micro-teaching framework will, in itself, raise interesting issues. For example, distinctions can be made between: (1) general teaching skills, applicable across all content areas, (2) teaching skills which are specific to certain subject matter, (3) teaching styles (inductive versus deductive, teacher-centered versus student-centered). Not only can such criteria be defined and re-examined in the microteaching setting, but questions of sequencing and prerequisites for teaching skills and styles can be settled.

7-5 APTITUDE-TREATMENT INTERACTIONS

One of the most exciting possibilities for research through micro-teaching is one which has been alluded to throughout this chapter and which could well serve as a unifying perspective in all such research. For an embarrassingly long period of time, educators have said much but done little about individualizing instruction. The standard approach, particularly in teacher education, has been for all students to take the same courses, have the same field experiences, be evaluated in the same way, and spend an equal amount of time acquiring credentials. But such packaged curricula are rapidly becoming outmoded at all levels of education. Different students obviously learn in different ways. To require them all to learn by the same set of experiences is at best inefficient and at worst stifling.

If, for example, we become so narrow in our applications of the techniques of microteaching that we require all teachers to learn the same skills in the same order and through the same training techniques, then we will overlook a powerful hidden resource of the microteaching process as a training and research vehicle. Thus an important research emphasis of microteaching is applying, within the microteaching framework, alternate training schemes that have been found valuable for teacher trainees whose characteristics, quite naturally, differ at the outset. Microteaching should be used as a research tool to determine the optimal training strategies for teacher trainees with different backgrounds and aptitudes. At the same time it should be used as a training strategy to give individual teachers the kind of training most suited to their particular abilities.

Here is one case of the possible interaction between the teacher trainees' aptitude and a particular microteaching treatment: Suppose we want to know what the training potential is of a videotaped model of a certain skill, as used in the training sessions of a microteaching clinic, versus a written description of the skill. People who design teacher training curricula usually go on the assumption that one or the other of those two procedures is best for all teacher trainees. The aspect that needs investigation is that for teacher trainees with certain aptitudes, the videotape model would be a more efficient training device than the written description, but that for teacher trainees with other aptitudes the written description would be more effective. For example, trainees with high verbal aptitudes might learn better from a written description, whereas trainees with low verbal aptitudes might learn better from a videotape model. The point is that the micro-teaching situation provides the opportunity both for investigating such questions and for implementing the results. Microteaching clinics could also determine whether different trainee aptitudes are related to different levels of progress in various training situations. If so, future micro-teaching clinics could provide different training procedures for trainees with different aptitudes, while at the same time gathering empirical evidence about how those training procedures could be refined to adapt themselves even more closely to individual differences. Thus we could use the microteaching framework to find and refine these aptitude-treatment interactions, and also to provide instruction capitalizing on those interactions that give teacher trainees the kinds of experiences best suited to their individual needs.

An additional category of research related to the microteaching framework may well be important in the near future: We do not know what the structure and sequence of microteaching in the teacher education program should be. When and for which purposes should micro-teaching be used in a teacher trainee's education? Very early, as a safe setting for preliminary teaching experience? Very late, as a specific skill training setting? What effect on a teacher's *real* classroom teaching (e.g., discipline problems, administrative behavior) does microteaching have? How can teachers use the microteaching setting as a basis for developing and evaluating curricula through a step-by-step process? What educational benefits to students could be engendered by providing them with opportunities for *teaching,* or being students in, different kinds of microteaching settings? What effect does a teacher's knowledge of his student's abilities and interests have on his teaching behavior in a micro-teaching session?

Here, as before, such questions suggest only a few of the alternatives open to those who wish to consider the research potential of the microteaching framework.

7-6 SUMMARY

This chapter is by no means comprehensive in its coverage of the research possibilities of microteaching. We have tried only to be heuristic and exemplary, suggesting some of the areas of research for which microteaching seems particularly suited. The following areas seem to make the most effective use of the microteaching setting: (1) in-house studies designed to optimize the procedures and sequences in the microteaching situation, (2) research in modeling and supervisory techniques, (3) task analyses of the teaching act and investigation of the relationship between teaching behaviors and student performance, (4) aptitude-treatment interaction studies, to try to provide optimal training procedures for teachers with different abilities, interests, and backgrounds.

It should be noted, of course, that these are merely areas which stand out as fields in which research is needed. But the most promising thing about microteaching as a research device is the extent to which it lends itself to new implementations and as-yet-unconceived experimental studies. Microteaching is one of the few experimental techniques which by its very structure encourages the combination of theory and practice, research and training, innovation and implementation. It is by this capacity for self-regulation that microteaching can perhaps revolutionize education. Research and training in the microteaching framework can build on one another. Therefore this new medium for teacher education may have as strong an impact on education as the techniques of culturing bacteria did in medicine. In the history of many sciences the development of new technology has created a new cycle of new research possibilities. We believe that microteaching may well be such a catalyst in education.

REFERENCES

1. Bandura, Albert, and Richard Walters, *Social Learning and Personality Development.* New York: Holt, Rinehart, and Winston, 1963.

2. Berlyne, D. E., *Conflict Arousal and Curiosity.* New York: McGraw-Hill, 1960.

3. Sokolov, E. N., "Neuronal Models and the Orienting Reflex," in *The Central Nervous System and Behavior,* edited by M. A. B. Brazier. New York: The Josiah Macy Foundation, 1960.

Bibliography

Acheson, Keith A., *The Effects of Feedback from Television Recordings and Three Types of Supervisory Treatment on Selected Teacher Behaviors.* Unpublished dissertation, Stanford University school of education, 1964

Allen, Dwight W., *Microteaching: A Description.* Stanford University school of education publication, 1967

Allen, Dwight W., Frederick J. McDonald, and Michael E.J. Orme, *Effects of Feedback and Practice Conditions on the Acquisition of a Teaching Strategy.* Mimeographed paper, Stanford University school of education, 1966

Allen, Dwight W., and Kevin A. Ryan, *A Perspective on the Education of Teachers in California in 1980.* Sacramento, Calif.: State of California Department of Education, State Committee on Public Education, November 1966

Allen, Dwight W., and David B. Young, *Television Recordings: A New Dimension in Teacher Education.* Mimeographed paper, Stanford University school of education, 1966

Ashlock, R. B., "Microteaching in an Elementary Science Methods Course," *School Science and Mathematics* **68**, January 1968, 52-56

Aubertine, Horace E., *The Use of Microteaching in the Process of Training Clinical Supervisors,* paper read at 1967 AERA Conference, New York

Aubertine, Horace E., "The Use of Microteaching in Training Supervising Teachers," *High School Journal* **51**, November 1967, 99-106

Belt, W. Dwayne, *Microteaching: Observed and Critiqued by a Group of Trainees vs. One Instructor and One Trainee,* paper read at AERA Conference, New York

Berliner, David C., *A Comparison of Different Modeling Procedures in the Acquisition of a Teaching Skill,* paper presented at 1967 AERA Conference, New York

Brigham Young University, *Microteaching at Brigham Young University.* Mimeographed paper, Provo, Utah: Brigham Young University, 1966

Bush, Robert N., and Dwight W. Allen, *Microteaching: Controlled Practices in the Training of Teachers,* paper presented at Santa Barbara Conference of Teacher Education, Ford Foundation, April 30, 1964

Clark, R. J., Jr., "Microteaching: Its Rationale," *High School Journal* **51**, November 1967, 75-79

Cook, F. S., and D. P. Brown, "Does Microteaching Have a Place in Business Education?" *Business Education World* **48**, April 1968

Cooper, James M., "Developing Teaching Skills Through Microteaching," *High School Journal* **51**, November 1967, 80-85

Cooper, James M., *Microteaching as a Pre-Internship Training Technique for the Development of Specific Teaching Skills,* paper read at 1967 AERA Conference, New York

Cyphert, Frederick R., *Video Recordings: The Most Desirable Tool for a Specific Job,* paper read at 1967 AERA Conference, New York

Dugas, D. G., "Microteaching: A Promising Medium for Teaching Retraining," *Modern Language Journal* **51**, March 1967, 161-166

Eggers, J. R., "Videotape Microteaching in 1-A Teacher Education," *Scholastic Shop* **27**, April 1968, 96-97

Fortune, Jimmie C., *Instructional Set, Cognitive Closure, and Test Anxiety in the Presentation of Social Studies Content.* Unpublished dissertation, Stanford University school of education, 1965

Fortune, Jimmie C., J. M. Cooper, and D. W. Allen, "The Stanford Summer Microteaching Clinic, 1965," *The Journal of Teacher Education* **18**, Winter 1967, 389-393

Foster, F. G., "Microteaching," *Arizona Teacher* **55**, May 1967, 12-13

Gross, R. E., "Microteaching: A New Beginning for Beginners," *NEA Journal* **55**, December 1965, 25-26

Johnson, W. D., "Microteaching: A Medium in Which to Study Teaching," *High School Journal* **51**, November 1967, 86-92

Johnson, W. D., *Microteaching: A Context for Studying Teaching Techniques,* paper read at 1967 AERA Conference, New York

Kallenbach, Warren, "Microteaching as a Teaching Methodology," *Proceedings: Conference on Instructional Methods and Teacher Behavior,*

Berkeley, Calif., Far West Laboratory for Educational Research and Development, 1966

Kallenbach, Warren, "The Effectiveness of Televised Student Teaching in the Preparation of Elementary Intern Teachers," *Technical Progress Report*, U.S. Office Grant No. 6-1303, mimeographed paper, San Jose State College school of education, 1967

Kallenbach, Warren, and Robert Ramonda, *The Effectiveness of Microteaching in the Preparation of Elementary Intern Teachers*, mimeographed paper, San Jose State College school of education, 1967

Mayhugh, S. L., "Microteaching: A Major Component of the Pre-Service Program," *Contemporary Education* 39, March 1968, 206-209

McDonald, Frederick J., D. W. Allen, and M. E. Orme, *The Effects of Self-Feedback and Reinforcement on the Acquisition of a Teaching Skill*, paper read at 1966 AERA Conference, Chicago

Meier, John H., *Remote Control Supervision of Teachers Using Video Recordings*, paper read at 1967 AERA Conference, New York

Olivero, James L., *Video Recordings as a Substitute for Live Observations in Teacher Education*. Unpublished dissertation, Stanford University school of education, 1964

Orme, Michael E.J., *The Effects of Modeling and Feedback Variables on the Acquisition of a Complex Teaching Strategy*. Unpublished dissertation, Stanford University school of education, 1964

Ramonda, Robert, "The Effectiveness of Microteaching in the Preparation of Elementary Intern Teachers: A Pilot Study," *Newsletter*, Phi Delta Kappa, San Jose State College, spring 1967

Ryan, Kevin A., *The Use of Students' Written Feedback in Changing the Behavior of Beginning Secondary School Teachers*. Unpublished dissertation, Stanford University school of education, 1966

Schaefer, M., and M. H. Stromquist, "Microteaching at Eastern Illinois University," *Audiovisual Instruction* 12, December 1967, 1064-1065

Sedgwick, L. K., and H. T. Misfeldt, "Microteaching: New Tool for a New Program," *Industrial Arts and Vocational Education* 56, June 1967, 34-35

Appendix*

The following material is reprinted from *Teaching Skills for Elementary and Secondary School Teachers,* a program consisting of short films and instruction manuals by Dwight W. Allen, Kevin Ryan, Robert N. Bush, and James Cooper, published by General Learning Corporation. Designed to facilitate observation and practice of techniques demonstrated by master teachers, the program may find use not only in microteaching, but also in the standard supervisor-teacher relationship, peer teaching, collegial supervision, and other formats.

REINFORCEMENT

A teacher plays a key role in the creation of desirable learning conditions in the classroom. As Sears and Hilgard have said:

> First, teacher personality and behavior act through a kind of contagion, in which the teacher becomes a model for appropriate behavior. The principles at work here are those of imitation and identification. Second, the teacher, as an administrator of rewards and punishments, wields power and creates a structure in which learning occurs. Here the principles are the more usual ones of positive and negative reinforcement.[1]

---

1 Pauline S. Sears and Ernest R. Hilgard, "The Teacher's Role in the Motivation of the Learner," *Theories of Learning and Instruction, The Sixty-third Yearbook of the National Society for the Study of Education, Part I* (Chicago, 1964), p. 206.

The teacher's role as a positive reinforcer is the focus of this exercise. Positive reinforcement of a behavior increases the likelihood that the behavior will recur. If a student behaves in a desirable way, immediate positive reinforcement increases the likelihood of his continuing to do so.

The difficulty is that the strength and quality of any reinforcer varies with the student to whom it is applied. No teacher can know exactly what will positively reinforce each of the thirty or so students in each of his five or six classes. It is impossible for him to acquire this information from the science of behavior at its present stage of development. Tests may eventually be developed to furnish such information, but that day is a long way off. Hence, the contemporary teacher must rely primarily on the words, phrases, and gestures that experience has shown to work as reinforcers in most cases. In addition, he should notice his students' individual traits. These will suggest that certain reinforcers might be more effective than others.

Besides directly increasing learning, reinforcement is an effective means of increasing student participation in classroom activities. Participation, in turn, usually increases learning. When students participate in classroom activities, they are more likely to become involved with the material than when they do not participate. They pay closer attention. An experiment conducted at Stanford University has shown that teachers who often reinforce their students for participating in class discussions draw more participation from their students than teachers who reinforce infrequently.[2] If teachers who use few reinforcement techniques in class discussions increase their use and range of techniques, they should significantly increase their students' participation.

Four kinds of positive reinforcement are available to the teacher:

1. Positive verbal reinforcement occurs when the teacher immediately follows a desired student response with such comments as

---

2   F. J. McDonald, D. W. Allen, and M. E. J. Orme, "The Effects of Self Feedback and Reinforcement on the Acquisition of a Teaching Skill," School of Education, Stanford University, 1967.

"Good," "Fine," "Excellent," "Correct," or other statements indicating satisfaction with the response.

2. Positive nonverbal reinforcement occurs when the teacher, in responding to a desired student response, nods his head affirmatively, smiles, moves toward the student, or keeps his eyes on the student while paying close attention to the student's words. The teacher may write the student's response on the chalkboard or otherwise nonverbally indicate pleasure at the student's response.

3. Positively qualified reinforcement occurs when the teacher differentially reinforces, either verbally or nonverbally, the acceptable parts of a response, as in the following example:

Teacher: John, how is yellow fever transmitted?

John: I think it is transmitted by flies.

Teacher: You're right, it's an insect that carries the disease, but it isn't a fly. What is it?

4. Delayed reinforcement occurs when the teacher emphasizes positive aspects of students' responses by redirecting class attention to earlier contributions by a student, as in this example:

Teacher: Class, which side would you have expected the English industrialists to support during the Civil War: the South or the North?

Class: The South. The North. (Class is divided)

Teacher: Jane, do you remember earlier in the class you mentioned one of the leading industries in England?

Jane: Yes. It was clothes-making.

Teacher: Does that give anyone a hint?

Sam: They supported the South because they wanted the cotton the South grew for making clothes.

Teacher: Good, Sam. That was a good deduction.

Note here that both Jane and Sam have been reinforced by the teacher: Jane, because the teacher drew the students' attention to her earlier contribution and asked her to repeat her statement; Sam, because the teacher praised him for deducing the answer to the original question.

Shy students who rarely participate in class discussion present a difficult problem, but not an insoluble one. Gradually, these students can be encouraged to participate. When a teacher notices a shy student looking at him or attending to what is going on in class, the teacher should reinforce this behavior by nodding or smiling at the student; in effect, the teacher says he is pleased that the student is paying attention. The teacher can further encourage this student's participation by asking him easy questions. This insures that the student will have successful experiences when he first begins to participate. If the teacher extends this process over a period of time, the student should participate more. Each time he participates, he should be reinforced, until he reaches a normal level of participation.

Most of us, in our normal conversations, use a very narrow range of reinforcers. "Good," "Uh-huh," "Right," and "Yeah," are frequently used as reinforcers. It is hoped that this exercise will enable you to extend your range of both verbal and nonverbal reinforcers. The possible range is a very broad one. It extends from such exclamations as "fantastic!" and "tremendous!" through statements such as "excellent," "very good," "good," and "yes," to mild gestures such as a slight nod of the head. Each of these reinforcers should convey a different feeling and meaning. Your task is to enlarge your repertoire of reinforcers and to apply them sensitively. Saying "tremendous!" to an average response, or even to a very good response, is ridiculous. Reinforcement must correspond to the adequacy of the student's response. A few of the reinforcing statements and actions outlined in the practice exercises may feel uncomfortable to you at first. They may seem foreign to your interaction style. However, as you develop your range of reinforcers, you should, in the long run, have a greater effect on your students.

TYPESCRIPT OF GLC FILM ON REINFORCEMENT

The four elementary school students are Cliff, Melissa, Darryl, and Sandra.

Teacher: Boys and girls, tomorrow we're going to start studying a new state which you haven't looked at before; and today I want to see if you can develop some good guesses about what kind of occupations we're going to find in this state. I've drawn a map for you; let me describe it briefly. We have the ocean on this side, coming into a bay. Most of the people—the majority of the people—live around this bay. We have rivers coming out; we have railroads leading down from the woods and from the mountains; and we have major highways going this way, and running along in this direction. Now, looking at the map, what kind of guesses do you have about what kind of jobs we're going to find in this state? Go ahead, Sandy.

Sandy: Fishermen.

Teacher: Why do you say so? *(Teacher nods head and smiles.)*

The teacher encourages the student by smiling and nodding.

Sandy: Because of the bay and the ocean.

Teacher: All right, good, good. Cliff, go ahead. *(Teacher writes "fishing" on board.)*

By writing the student's comment on the board, the teacher publicly recognizes that the student has made a valuable contribution. Note that the teacher does this several times during the lesson.

Cliff: Boating in the bay—there would be boating in the bay or sailing.

Teacher: Uh, I think that's probably a good idea. Why do you say so?

Cliff: Because of the bay.

Comments

Teacher: The . . . the bay is . . . is, uh, protected enough? *(Teacher smiles at Cliff.)*

Cliff: Um-hum.

Teacher: All right. Fine. *(Teacher writes "boating" on board.)* Go ahead, Darryl. *(Teacher smiles at Darryl.)*

Darryl: Um, well, um, lumberjacks and because um, 'cause they'll need wood to burn and to put . . . *(Teacher listens intently and steps closer to Darryl as he talks.)*

As the student speaks, the teacher gives him undivided attention, listening closely to what the student is saying.

Teacher: Okay, now hold on here a minute. You've got a good idea going. Now why do you say lumberjacks?

Darryl: Because well, um . . . the trees and in the sort of forest and . . . *(Teacher nods his head.)*

Teacher: Good, you're doing very well. Do you see anything else around the woods that would lead you to think that they do some lumbering up there? Or can someone else take Darryl's idea and build on that from there? Sandy. *(Teacher writes "lumberjacks" on board.)*

Sandy: The railroads, they . . . they send the logs to the factories by railway.

Teacher: All right, very good. You're building on Darryl's idea, and I think that's a . . . that's a very good point to make. Now let's keep going with Darryl's idea for just a minute. Where you have lumberjacks and where you have forest and logs going to a factory, what else might you expect to find? Darryl? *(Teacher smiles and steps closer to Darryl.)*

The teacher throughout the lesson builds a feeling of group involvement in trying to solve the problem. He does this by trying to get students to build upon one another's ideas. Watch for this during the lesson.

Darryl: Um, well, they need the sawmill to . . . sand the, um, the wood out so you won't get, you know, much scratches like usually when you first take a piece of wood, you scrub your hand on it and you get a splinter . . .

Teacher: Okay, you're doing fine. *(Teacher nods and writes "etc." after lumberjacks.)*

Darryl: . . . in your finger.

Teacher: We have other things, then, associated with the lumberjacks. Good, you're taking your own idea and doing something with it. Cliff?

Cliff: Tourism in the city.

Teacher: Very interesting.

Positive verbal reinforcement.

Cliff: Because of all the stores.

Teacher: Because of all the stores in the city is why you have tourism?

Cliff: Especially the ladies, because they like to look through the stores. *(Teacher smiles and laughs.)*

Teacher: All right. Uh, Cliff's got a good idea. Can you see other reasons why we might find tourism? Maybe some better ideas than Cliff had on it. Go ahead, Sandy.

Here is an example of a positively qualified reinforcement. Cliff has given a good idea, but his reason for it is not the best. The teacher rewards Cliff for his contribution but also qualifies his acceptance of Cliff's reason. The teacher then seeks to get other students to supply good reasons for Cliff's idea.

Sandy: Well, there could be snow in the mountains, and they could ski . . .

Teacher: All right, another reason . . .

Sandy: . . . and bobsled.

Teacher: . . . for Cliff's idea . . . Melissa, you had another reason?

Melissa: Well, maybe because of the bay, you know, some people like maybe to do boating or something. *(Teacher writes "tourism" on board.)*

Teacher: That's excellent. We took Cliff's idea and we got at least two other reasons why that idea was a good one. I think we're doing fine. Darryl, go ahead.

Notice the group reinforcement as opposed to just reinforcing individual students.

Darryl: Um, well, there is one other idea, um . . . I think, um, gold mining in the mountains. *(Teacher listens intently.)*

Teacher: All right—keep going, why? *(Teacher nods his head in agreement.)*

The teacher encourages Darryl.

Darryl: Um, because, um, well they'd be trying to find the mine . . . I mean, they'd go in the mines and, um, they'd start hauling stuff like . . . *(Teacher writes "mining" on board.)*

Teacher: Okay, but now, Darryl, hold on a minute. You got a good idea going here, but I'm not sure that you're giving the right reasons for it. What do you see on here that makes you think we're going to find gold mining, or mining in general?

Another example of a qualified reinforcement. By supplying Darryl with clues the teacher tries to get Darryl to justify his answer.

Darryl: Well there is a lot of coal in the mountains . . .

Teacher: All right.

Darryl: . . . and . . .

Teacher: You're saying it right there, I think you see mountains.

Darryl: Yeah.

Teacher: Where you see mountains, you think you'll probably find some mining. Does anything else here suggest that you might find lots of things going on in the mountains? Go ahead, Sandy.

Sandy: The railways again, they . . . send things . . . *(Teacher nods head.)*

Teacher: Excellent . . . fine, and perhaps this as well. All right, other ideas? You're doing real well. You might want to take a look at some of the things you've said over here and forget about the map for just a minute. Build on your own ideas. Sandy has suggested we'd find fishermen; Cliff, you suggested that we'd find sailing going on here; here are some other things that have been suggested. Now, where we have these, what else might we find here? Melissa, go ahead.

This is a good example of delayed reinforcement. By reminding the class of students' past contributions, the teacher reinforces these students.

Melissa: I'm not sure this is right, but you know, people would be working on bridges, you know, to . . . uh, you know, at the end or something for people to pay their way.

Teacher: Good, I think that's an interesting idea. Do you think, uh, it will be one of these? *(Teacher underlines the word "major" under "major occupations.")*

Another example of a qualified reinforcement. Note that the teacher does not reject Melissa's contribution, but he still gets her to question whether her answer is really a major occupation.

Melissa: Well, uh, I . . .

Teacher: Lots and lots of people doing it.

Melissa: . . . guess so. I don't know.

Teacher: All right. We'll put this down—bridge-building, with a question mark, listed here. *(Teacher writes "bridge building" on board.)* I know you have some other ideas—this is great—and you've taken . . . you've taken each others' ideas from what you've seen here and really built well with them. Tomorrow, when we get started, we'll have a chance to expand this some, and then you'll have a chance to go into the books and test how good your ideas really are. I think you're going to be surprised at how good your guesses are. Very good job. *(Teacher nods head and smiles at students.)* Again, good use of group reinforcement techniques.

EVALUATION SHEET: REINFORCEMENT

Students, supervisors, and teachers:

1. When a student answered a question correctly or asked a good question, did the teacher reward him with such words as "Fine," "Good," "Excellent," etc.?
   List the words he used and the number of times he used each:

2. What nonverbal cues (e.g., a smile or a nod of the head) did the teacher use to encourage his students?

3. When a student gave an answer that was only partially correct, did the teacher give him credit for the correct part?

4. Did the teacher ever refer to the positive aspects of a student's previous response?

Comments:

SKILL DRILL: REINFORCEMENT

Directions: Listed below are a number of classroom situations in which student responses require some kind of reinforcement. After studying each of the situations, write the reinforcing comment(s) you would make and any nonverbal reinforcement you would use. Think up three different reinforcers for each situation. Do not use a reinforcement you have used for a previous situation. Practice a variety.

Situation 1: You have been discussing with the class the technique for bisecting an angle. For the last fifteen minutes you have been circulating around the room while the students practiced the technique. You arrive at John's chair. He is a C— student who is easily discouraged. He has completed more practice exercises than anyone else, and all of them are neat and correct. John looks up and asks, "Teacher, how are these?"

1.

2.

3.

Situation 2: Three weeks ago you assigned book reports. They were turned in yesterday. Last night you read five. Among them was one by Sue, one of the brightest girls in the class. It was an analytical essay on Joseph Conrad's *Lord Jim.* It was well written and quite perceptive. Today, before the class begins, you are sitting at your desk when Sue walks into the room.

1.

2.

3.

Situation 3: During a class discussion, a shy, withdrawn student named Jim starts to raise his hand to make a comment, but then changes his mind and lowers his hand.

1.

2.

3.

Situation 4: During a class discussion, Mary, an average student with no known emotional problems, attempts to answer a question. Her answer is generally on the right track, but it includes several errors.

1.

2.

3.

Situation 5: You are handing back a homework assignment. When you get to Sue, you remember that she didn't do very well on it. She seemed to have ignored some basic points. You have been concerned with her work for some time, for it has been sloppy and irregular.

1.

2.

3.

Situation 6: During a class discussion, Kim asks a very pertinent question. You remember that Frank wrote a report last semester on that very topic. (Reinforce both students.)

·1.

2.

3.

Situation 7: A student is attempting to answer a question you asked the class. He is doing a good job, and you want him to know that you think it's a good answer. But you don't want to interrupt him.

1.

2.

3.

Situation 8: Alex has come up to your desk after class and volunteered to do an oral report on an esoteric topic mentioned briefly in class. He doesn't usually do this sort of thing. You want to take advantage of his interest.

1.

2.

3.

SILENCE AND NONVERBAL CUES

Most teachers tend to think that verbal communication is the best way to increase student participation. Although this is important, the teacher's use of silence and nonverbal communication can also be effective.

Usually it is the students who use silence (sometimes intentionally and sometimes not) to control the teacher's behavior. For example, the teacher asks a student a question, but the student says nothing and looks uncomfortable. The teacher, himself now uncomfortable, breaks the silence by speaking. He may reword the question, elaborate on it, or ask it of another student. Through the use of silence, the student has forced the teacher to keep talking. In such a situation, the students control the teacher.

It is possible, however, for the teacher to take advantage of silence. The object of this exercise is to practice the use of silence and some nonverbal cues to increase student participation. In behavioral terms, this means increasing the amount of student participation by decreasing the amount of teacher talk.

After an introductory statement, silence stimulates students to think about what the teacher has just said. The silence suggests that the statement is important.

After a question from a student, silence indicates that the teacher is considering the question. At the same time, silence suggests to the students that they, too, should be considering the question. After a momentary silence, the teacher answers the question or, better yet, redirects it to another student through the use of a nod, a gesture, or a look.

Silence is often appropriate *after asking a student a question.* It is often frustrating to a student to be asked a question and not given time to formulate an answer. He frequently finds himself passed over for one of the students who is frantically waving his hand at the teacher to indicate that he knows the answer. The teacher should always pause to give the student time to think, even if doing so causes the teacher to endure an uncomfortable silence.

After a student response, silence will encourage the student to continue talking. Students are frequently satisfied with single-statement answers. But, through the use of silence, the teacher fosters an extended, elaborated response.

Because of its ambiguity, however, mere silence is not enough to effectively control student participation. The student cannot always tell from mere silence whether the teacher is indicating acceptance, rejection, or thoughtful consideration. Therefore, silence is most effective when accompanied by a nonverbal cue indicating pleasure, displeasure, questioning, acceptance, or rejection.

Four main kinds of nonverbal cues will be considered in this exercise. *Facial cues* are the easiest for students to detect, and thus are often the most powerful. A smile directed toward a responding student encourages him and indicates the teacher's desire that the student continue. A frown indicates displeasure with the student's response. A frown may have one of two effects: it may halt the student's response or it may stimulate him to justify or clarify his response. If the teacher remains silent after frowning, the student will probably feel uncomfortable enough to elaborate on his answer. There are a number of other facial expressions that cue the student: (1) looking thoughtful as the student responds indicates that the teacher is seriously considering the response; (2) continuing to look seriously at the student while he is responding usually encourages him to continue talking; and (3) looking quizzically at the student, as though his answer were not clear, usually stimulates him to reword his answer or elaborate upon it. In all of these instances, the combined use of silence and nonverbal cues will probably encourage the student to continue talking or encourage other students to respond.

A second kind of nonverbal cue is *head movement.* While the teacher listens to a student, he can encourage the student with a smile or with a nod of his head. Nodding indicates to the student that he is at least on the right track. In the same manner, a shake of the teacher's head indicates that the student is on the wrong track. It may cause the student to change his response. Another head movement is the cocked ear. By tilting his head and ear toward the student and assuming a thoughtful look, the teacher says, in effect, that he is listening to the student.

Body movement is a third kind of nonverbal cue. By moving near the student when he is responding, the teacher indicates that he wants to hear what the student is saying. This kind of movement encourages the student. Assuming a thoughtful pose (fist under chin, for example) indicates to the class that the teacher is considering the student's statement.

The nonverbal cues mentioned above should not be considered separate, discrete actions, but rather parts of a behavior pattern. Facial, body, and head movements are combined in patterns to increase student participation. Patterned behavior can be seen most clearly in the use of *gestures,* such as the following:

1. Pointing to student: Rather than call the student by name, the teacher can merely point to him and smile or nod his head.

2. "Continue" cue: Moving the hands in a circular motion similar to a wheel will indicate to the student that he should continue, that he's on the right track. This gesture should normally be accompanied by a smile, a nod of encouragement, a movement toward the student, or any combination of these.

3. "Anything else?" cue: By holding the hands out with the palms upward, while looking quizzically or expectantly at the student, the teacher seems to be asking the question, "Is there anything else?"

4. "Stop" cue: By holding the arm straight out with the hand up and the palm out, the teacher can halt an irrelevant or incorrect response, cause a student to reconsider his words, or give himself more time to consider the student's response.

5. Pointing from student to student: To elicit student-to-student interaction the teacher can first point to one student and then to the student who has just finished responding, and then look quizzically back and forth from one to the other. This indicates to the first student that the teacher wants him to respond to the other's comment.

Although the teacher will try to say as little as possible during his microteaching practice, for the purpose of acquiring skill in the use of silence and nonverbal cues, it is unlikely that in an actual classroom he would remain silent for long periods of time. He would in most cases interspace his nonverbal cues and silence with selected comments. He should not overuse silence. If he does, silence will cease to be effective, just as talking when overused, ceases to be effective. Communication patterns should vary.

TYPESCRIPT OF GLC FILM
ON SILENCE AND NONVERBAL CUES

The four elementary school students are Hila, Doug, Teya, and Geoff.

Teacher: I noticed in the papers this morning a report of a study that said cigarette smoking is linked with cancer. Another study not too long ago said something about cigarette smoking being connected with heart disease, and yet I look around me on my way to work, and I see lots and lots and lots of people smoking. I want to ask you people two questions: (1) why they smoke, and (2) what might be done to stop it, if it is harmful to health. *(Teacher puts finger to mouth and looks thoughtful. He then turns to Hila and looks at her.)*
(PAUSE)

This is the last time the teacher says anything until he summarizes at the end.

By looking at Hila, the teacher conveys an expectation that Hila will say something. She senses this and responds to his expectation.

The nonverbal cues are encouraging. Hila continues to speak and elaborate on her answer.

Hila: Well, they could have a law against it *(teacher nods head and encourages her to continue speaking by motioning with his hand),* but that's something kind of hard to do because not all people are for the law; even though they're discussing it, not all people want the law. *(Teacher nods his head, then turns and looks at Geoff.)*

By looking at Geoff the teacher conveys his expectation that Geoff will participate. Geoff senses this and makes a contribution.

Geoff: Well, if we had the law ... um, people would probably break it *(teacher nods his head and encourages Geoff to continue speaking by motioning with his hand)*—they'd probably break the law; and if they made a law against making cigarettes, they'd ... no one could keep 'em from making them, like in a cellar or something—like the law that was passed in the United States about, um, wine. *(Teacher looks puzzled and scratches his head.)* It was passed that you aren't supposed to sell wine, but people made it—got sick from making it. *(Teacher laughs and nods his head indicating understanding and acceptance of Geoff's answer. He then looks at Teya and motions with his hand, encouraging her to speak.)*

The teacher expresses puzzlement over what Geoff has said. Geoff recognizes this and elaborates on his answer. The teacher's look and gesture perform the same function as a probing question by getting the student to go beyond the initial information he has already given. Note that the teacher is quite warm and receptive to the student's comments. He creates a situation in which the students are comfortable and do not feel threatened. Such an atmosphere is essential if the teacher is seeking student participation.

Teya: Well I don't ... I think that, um, people probably wouldn't give it up, even ... some people—most people would if there was a law, but some people really like cigarettes. I mean lots of people like cigarettes *(teacher nods head)*—they find that cigarettes is kind of a fun way ... well, it's kind of an interesting thing—it's just ... it appeals to them; and the taste is kind of interesting and different *(teacher nods head and smiles)*, so that they smoke; and they might not want to give it up. So what do they do? They break the law, just like marijuana and things have been passed—you can't have this unless the doctors prescribe it, but people break the laws. *(Teacher looks puzzled and holds out his hand indicating to Teya to stop talking for a moment while he thinks over her answer. After a few moments he nods his head and indicates with his hand that she should continue speaking. As she starts to speak, he leans forward and listens intently to what she says).* (PAUSE) Well, people, I mean, just, um, sometimes they don't want to give up what they've got, and they think it's interesting and it's a good kick—it's really something that they enjoy—they aren't going to give it up. *(Teacher smiles and nods his head. He then looks at Doug, leans foward and cups his ear with his finger.)*

This sequence of behaviors indicates that the teacher is still directing the discussion; it has not gotten away from him. Teya stopped right in the middle of a train of thought while the teacher thought over her previous statements. When he had satisfied himself as to her answer, he asked her through hand motions to continue speaking.

Doug: People like smoking—they think it's nice. *(Teacher nods head.)* Well, it gives them something to do. *(Nods head vigorously, smiles.)*

Geoff: And well, to answer your other question, some people can't quit because they smoked most of their lives from the . . . maybe the Second World War *(teacher nods head and encourages Geoff to continue speaking by motioning with his hand),* they started having cigarettes and the soldiers smoked them and some of the other people would get them and smoke them and would make it so that they couldn't stop. Even if they hated the way it tasted, some people still couldn't stop smoking it. *(Teacher laughs and nods head. He then looks around at students, settling on Hila. He raises his eyebrow as if to say, "Do you have something to say?")*

This movement of the eyebrows also conveys an expectation on the teacher's part that the student will say something.

Hila: Well, they could have a law that, uh, from like tomorrow on *(teacher looks quizzically at Hila)*—from a week past tomorrow—no smoking would be allowed, and people are requested to make their smoking fewer and fewer cigarettes a day. *(Teacher strokes his beard while thinking about Hila's comments. He then nods his head in agreement.)* That would be kind of hard to keep track of *(teacher holds out hand as if to ask, "Why?")*, 'cause people can break it very easily. *(Teacher nods head and looks around at rest of students.)*

Teya: Well, they could have a law, I think, that said that no cigarettes could be made. I mean, not just saying that— saying that no cigarettes in America can be sold or anything like this. *(Teacher looks intently at Teya.)* That means that all these firms in America could be closed down so that no one could smoke even if they wanted to. *(Teacher motions from Teya to Hila and back again, looking at Hila as if to say, "What do you think about what she is saying?")*

Hila: Well, I just thought of something and that is, if no cigarettes would be, um, allowed . . . no one would be allowed to smoke cigarettes, the people who make cigarettes would get broke. *(Teacher looks at Teya and motions with his hand for her to respond to Hila's comments.)*

This time the hand motion from student to student has an effect, as Teya directs her remarks to Hila. This type of interaction should be encouraged by teachers. Also, notice that the seating arrangement helps facilitate this kind of student-to-student interaction.

Teya: But even then, um . . . yeah, but that's like what I said—it would be almost closing down the factories, so if they just said that the people who were in the cigarette factories couldn't make cigarettes any more—just not allowing cigarettes to be sold in America. *(Teacher nods his head, then looks at Geoff.)*

Geoff: Um, well still they could grow tobacco plants *(teacher looks puzzled and holds out hands as if to say, "What do you mean?")*, I mean how are you going to stop, um, farmers from growing tobacco plants in other countries? *(Teacher understands the point, smiles, and nods his head vigorously in agreement.)* You just go to another country and you pick up a crate of tobacco.

Teacher: Right, I think there would be a lot of people breaking a law like you say might go into effect. I think you see the complexity—first of all, you hit on the problems of why people smoke a little bit—it gives them some satisfaction; and the tremendous difficulty in deciding what to do about it—what kinds of laws, if any, can be passed.

Comments:

EVALUATION SHEET: SILENCE AND NONVERBAL CUES

Students, supervisors, and teachers:

1. Did the teacher allow the students to do most of the talking?

2. Did the teacher remain quiet after asking a question, thus allowing the student time to think about his answer?

3. Did the teacher communicate with facial expressions, gestures, and body movements?

4. Was the teacher able to direct and control the discussion without speaking very often?

5. Was the teacher attentive? Did the teacher seem interested in what the students had to say?

6. Did the teacher make an effort to include as many students as possible in the discussion?

Comments:

1. Did the teacher allow the students to do most of the talking?

Index

Perlberg, Arye, 102
Pinney, Robert, vi
Planned repetition, 15
Playbacks, video, 22
Politzer, Robert, vi
Practice teaching, 3-4
Prairie View A and M College, 104
Pre-instructional techniques, 18 ff
Pre-service teacher education programs,
   25, 38, 60 ff, 92
  and imitation, 60
  and microteaching clinic, 66-69
  and observation, 60
  at San Jose State College, 79
  and use of models, 32
Probing questions, 15
Program evaluation, 94

Qualified reinforcement, 133
Quirk, Tom, vi

Ramonda, Robert J., 79, 125
Recognizing attending behavior, 15,
   107
Recorders, videotape (*See* Videotape
   recorders)
Recruitment of microteaching students, 48
Reinforcement, 22, 54, 87, 126 ff
  delayed, 128, 133
  evaluation sheet for, 134
    group, 132
  positive nonverbal, 128
  positive verbal, 128
  positively qualified, 128
  qualified, 133
  skill drill in, 134 ff
  typescript of GLC film on, 129 ff
Reinforcement of student
   participation, 15, 27
Research clinical sessions, 38, 43-45
Research in education, 8, 110 ff
Resource personnel, 76
Reteach lessons, iv, 8, 27, 40, 93, 98,
   105
Robertson, Alan, v
Rogerian reflection of feeling, 107
Rogers, Carl, 107
Role-playing students, 11-12
Romney, A. Kimball, iv
Rosenshine, Borak, vi
Ryan, Kevin, vi, 88, 123, 125, 126

Ryan, Marilyn, viii
San Francisco State College, 65
San Jose State College, 79-82
  analysis of microteaching clinic at,
   82
Schaefer, M., 125
Schedules for microteaching clinics, 37
Sears, Pauline S., 126n
Sedgwick, L. K., 125
Seidman, Earl, vi
Selection of microteaching students,
   49
Sequence of events in microteaching,
   113
Set induction, 13, 15, 18 ff
Shifting sensory channels, as method
   of stimulus variation, 18
Shy students, problem of, 129
Silence, student use of, 139
  teacher use of, 139-140
Silence and nonverbal cues, 15, 20 ff,
   139 ff
  evaluation sheet for, 146
  typescript of GLC film on, 142 ff
Simon and Garfunkel, 74
Skills (*See* Teaching skills)
Sobol, Frank, vi
Social distance, correct, 63-64
Sokolov, E. N., 118
Southern University, 104
Specifics of teaching, vocabulary for, 5
Stanford Microteaching Clinic, 43, 45,
   53, 57
  description of, 78
Stanford Teacher Competency Ap-
   praisal Guide, 80
Stanford Teacher Education Program,
   iv, 4, 10, 14, 43, 79
Stanford University, iv, 4, 20n, 33, 43,
   49, 53, 59, 78, 104, 127n
  and Peace Corps training, 95
Stimulus variation, 15 ff, 105, 118
Stromquist, M. H., 125
Student behavior problems, 87
Student feedback forms, 3, 39, 52, 105
Student participation, 5, 21, 22, 127,
   143
Students, attitudes of, 48
  characteristics of, 112
  coordinator for, 53
  effect of clinic experience on, 54
  recruitment of, 48
  role of, in microteaching, 1, 47

selection of, 49
as sources of feedback, 53
Spanish-speaking, 100
training of, 50
Summarization of feeling, 107
Supervision, attitude of teachers toward, 7
focused on one skill, 24
in a microteaching setting, 7, 22, 111
primary aim of, 75
Supervisors, and benefits from microteaching, 65
clinically trained, 90-91
and the component-skills approach,
24
dual role of, 45
generalist vs. specialist, 25
inadequate training of, 89
in an in-service clinic, 77
part-time, 87
Peace Corps returnees as, 96-97
and research in human learning,
116-117
role of, in microteaching, 1, 8, 39,
45, 56
training of, 46 ff, 66
and videotape, 56

Teacher Aide Program, 10
Teacher Corps, 79
at Memphis State University, 92-94
Teachers, attitude toward supervisors, 7
as continuous learners, 6, 73
critical periods for, 66
difficulties of beginners, 61-65
lack of professional dialog among,
74-75
in-service training of, 6, 25, 76
and opportunities for practice, 3-4
outstanding, as models, 6
performance of, related to performance of pupils, 117-118
professional development of, 1, 4, 6,
68
and silence and nonverbal cues, 20
in urban public schools, 86-89
Teacher-training institutions, 25
Teaching, components of, 14 ff, 97
and effect on student learning, 119
Teaching English as a second language,
95 ff

Teaching skills, 5, 13 ff, 65, 71
closure, 19
examples of component, 15
isolation of different, 7, 23, 26
modeling of, 26
and Peace Corps, 97
reinforcement, 22
set induction, 18
silence and nonverbal cues, 20
stimulus variation, 15
Team-teaching approach, 43
Tennessee A and I State University,
104
Trainee teachers, and demonstration
teachers, 26 ff
initial difficulties of, 61
and the micro-lesson, 39
and microteaching, 3, 13, 118
reaction to videotape, 55
supervision of, 77
and supervisors, 45, 65
Tuskegee Institute, 104

Vanderbilt University, 104
Variation of stimulus (*See* Stimulus
variation)
Videotape, analysis of usefulness,
54-55
supervisors' use of, 56
use of, iv-v, 47, 62, 88, 97, 100, 112
Videotape recorders, not necessary for
microteaching, 54
operators of, 57-59, 77
and outstanding model teachers, 6
portable, 30, 55, 85
and training of teachers, iv-vi, 27, 55
as used in microteaching, 1, 54
Volunteers, in microteaching clinic,
101

Wagschal, Peter, viii
Wegner, Donna, vii
Wehmeyer, Donald, v, vi
Whitman College microteaching clinic,
89-92
Williamson, Merritt A., 104-105

Young, David B., vi, 104, 123